The Testaments of the Patriarchs

Secret Farewells & Prophetic Warnings of Ancient Israel

The Last Words of Abraham, Moses, Job, Solomon, and the Twelve Patriarchs

A Modern Translation

Adapted for the Contemporary Reader

Various Ancient Writers

Translated by Tim Zengerink

Table of Contents

Preface - Message to the Reader

What If You Could Help Rebuild the Greatest Library in Human History?

Thousands of years ago, the Library of Alexandria stood as the crown jewel of human achievement — a sanctuary where the collected wisdom of every known civilization was gathered, preserved, and shared freely.

And then, it was lost.

Through fire, conquest, and the slow erosion of time, humanity lost not just books — but ideas, dreams, discoveries, and stories that could have changed the world forever.

Today, the Library of Alexandria lives again — and you are invited to be a part of its restoration.

Our mission is simple yet profound:

To rebuild the greatest library the world has ever known, and to translate all timeless works into every language and dialect, so that no seeker of knowledge is ever left behind again.

By joining our movement to rebuild the modern Library of Alexandria, you become part of an unprecedented mission:

- **Unlimited Access to the Greatest Audiobooks & eBooks Ever Written:**

  Instantly explore thousands of legendary works—Plato, Shakespeare, Jane Austen, Leo Tolstoy, and countless more. All instantly available to read or listen, placing a complete literary universe at your fingertips.

- **Beautiful Paperback & Deluxe Editions at Printing Cost**

  Own any title as an elegant paperback, deluxe hardcover, or stunning collectible boxset—offered to you at true printing cost, delivered straight to your door. Build your personal Library of Alexandria, crafted for beauty, built for durability, and worthy of proud display.

- **Fresh Translations for Modern Readers—in Every Language & Dialect**

  Enjoy timeless masterpieces reimagined in clear, contemporary language—no more outdated phrases or obscure references. Alongside the original versions, we're tirelessly translating these classics into every language and dialect imaginable, ensuring accessibility and understanding across cultures and generations.

- **Join a Global Renaissance of Literature & Knowledge**

  You directly support expanding our library, publishing deluxe editions at true cost, translating works into all global languages, and bringing humanity's greatest stories to people everywhere. By joining today, you're not just preserving a legacy of masterpieces; you set in motion a powerful wave of literary accessibility.

Become a Torchbearer of Knowledge.

Join us for free now at **LibraryofAlexandria.com**

Together, we will ensure that the light of human wisdom never fades again.

With gratitude and a shared love of knowledge,

The Modern Library of Alexandria Team

Visit:

www.libraryofalexandria.com

Or scan the code below:

Introduction

The Final Words of Israel's Founding Fathers

Throughout the ancient world, the final words of a revered leader held profound weight. They were not merely parting thoughts, but enduring legacies—often packed with blessing, instruction, warning, and vision. For Israel, the patriarchs were more than family forebears; they were chosen vessels of divine revelation. Their last words were sacred inheritances, cherished and preserved for generations. The Testaments of the Patriarchs brings together these closing discourses—voiced by Abraham, Isaac, Jacob, Moses, Job, Solomon, and the twelve sons of Jacob—in one powerful collection that opens a window into the moral, spiritual, and prophetic consciousness of ancient Israel.

This anthology blends wisdom literature, ethical instruction, visionary experience, and messianic prophecy. It is both profoundly human and deeply theological. These texts are more than farewells—they are final commissions to a people poised between memory and destiny. Whether given from a deathbed, spoken in a final audience, or revealed through celestial visions, each testament seeks to transmit something urgent and sacred: a vision of how to live, what to expect, and how to remain faithful to the covenant in the trials to come.

The most prominent of these works—the Testaments of the Twelve Patriarchs—offers imagined deathbed speeches from each of Jacob's sons: Reuben, Simeon, Levi, Judah, Issachar, Zebulun, Dan, Naphtali, Gad, Asher, Joseph, and Benjamin. But this volume expands the scope further, including the Testament of Abraham, Isaac, and Jacob, the esoteric Testament of Solomon, the ethical-poetic Testament of Job, and the powerful prophetic voice of the Testament of Moses. In these texts, we find not only personal wisdom, but also insight into the spiritual imagination of early Judaism and the theological soil in which Christianity would take root.

Ethical Vision, Prophetic Expectation, and Celestial Testimony

The testaments follow a common pattern: an aged patriarch gathers his children or followers, often while bedridden, and recounts the course of his life—his struggles, sins, triumphs, and divine encounters. But they also move outward, offering commands, predictions, and visions meant to instruct future generations.

In the Testaments of the Twelve Patriarchs, each son of Jacob gives a monologue that blends autobiography with moral exhortation. Reuben confesses his sin and urges chastity; Simeon denounces envy; Levi speaks of priesthood and holiness; Judah tells of leadership and repentance. Each figure becomes a moral exemplar—sometimes through virtue, sometimes through failure. These texts lay out virtues such as humility, generosity, and loyalty, and condemn the vices that led Israel astray: lust, anger, deceit, and pride. They emphasize the power of repentance, the promise of God's mercy, and the consequences of rebellion. Collectively, they offer a spiritual mirror in which Israel might see both its past and its prophetic future.

The Testament of Moses similarly blends historical review with apocalyptic foresight. Moses reflects on Israel's journey, predicts the rise of a wicked priesthood, and foretells a future deliverer—a messianic figure who will restore righteousness. This text, likely written during the Hellenistic or early Roman period, mirrors the political pressures and prophetic yearnings of an oppressed people awaiting divine intervention.

The Testament of Job is unlike any other. Framed as Job's final instructions to his children, it retells the classic story with greater emphasis on Job's steadfast faith, visionary experiences, and mystical insights. Job is not only a man of patience but a spiritual hero—a contemplative, a prophet, and a model of integrity who triumphs not through conquest but endurance.

The Testament of Abraham, often humorous and deeply philosophical, explores questions of death, justice, and divine mercy. In a dreamlike narrative, Abraham is guided by angels through visions of judgment and celestial courts. His refusal to accept death reveals both his righteousness and his human hesitation before the unknown. Ultimately, Abraham consents to God's will, offering a model of surrender, trust, and divine intimacy.

The Testament of Solomon, on the other hand, moves into esoteric and mystical territory. Blending folklore, apocalyptic symbolism, and demonology, it tells how Solomon received a ring from heaven that gave him power to control spirits and build the Temple. Through a series of interrogations with demons and spiritual entities, Solomon learns their names, powers, and vulnerabilities. The text mixes moral instruction with spiritual warfare and is one of the earliest examples of Jewish magical literature.

Each of these works, while varying in tone and content, aims to preserve and transmit a sacred worldview: one in which human choices matter, history unfolds under divine supervision, and the soul's journey extends far beyond this life.

Spiritual Heritage and Contemporary Relevance

Why revisit these ancient farewell speeches today? In a fragmented world where faith, identity, and morality often seem disoriented, the testaments offer grounding. They remind us that the challenges we face—ethical dilemmas, societal decline, spiritual longing—are not new. The patriarchs too lived in turbulent times. They faced the temptation to compromise, the sorrow of loss, and the weight of legacy. In their final moments, they chose to teach, to warn, and to hope.

Their words remain relevant not only for their theological depth, but also for their profound human empathy. They speak to families, to leaders, to communities struggling to preserve wisdom in the face of change. They call us back to virtues that transcend eras: compassion, honesty, purity, reverence, and the pursuit of justice.

Moreover, these texts illuminate the bridges between Judaism and Christianity. The messianic hints in the Testaments of the Twelve Patriarchs, the angelic encounters in Abraham and Job, the heavenly visions in Moses and Ezra—these laid the groundwork for later Christian theology, particularly concerning the Messiah, resurrection, and divine judgment. The testaments were widely read in the Second Temple period and were preserved, quoted, and sometimes adapted by early Christians. Their themes resonate deeply with New Testament values while maintaining their distinct Jewish voice.

This volume is an invitation to listen—across centuries—to the dying words of the living faithful. As you encounter these testaments, may you be stirred not only by their solemnity but by their passion. May you hear in them not just the last breath of the past but the first breath of enduring wisdom. These patriarchs speak not only to their children but to all who seek truth, courage, and the faith to endure.

Let their voices awaken your own.

Testament of Adam

Introduction

The Testament of Adam is an ancient text that is said to have been written by Adam, the first man in the Bible. It has been preserved in different languages and gives a mystical and prophetic view of the universe, worship, and the future redemption of humanity. This text provides insight into early Jewish and Christian beliefs, combining religious ideas with visions of the end times.

The text focuses on three main ideas: the sacred hours of the day and night, Adam's prophecy about the coming of the Messiah, and a vision of the world's future. The first part explains how each hour of the day and night is dedicated to praising God—by angels, animals, heavenly beings, and even nature itself. This idea shows the harmony of creation and how God's presence is everywhere.

The second part contains a prophecy in which Adam predicts the coming of Christ. After being cast out of Paradise, Adam receives a promise from God that His Word will become human, be born from a virgin, and perform miracles to save people. This vision closely matches Christian beliefs about Jesus, making the Testament of Adam important for understanding early Christian ideas about the Messiah.

The final section describes the destruction and renewal of the world. Adam speaks of a great flood that will cleanse the earth because of the evil of Cain's descendants and also predicts that, in the end, the world will be purified by fire. These ideas are similar to themes found in biblical and other ancient texts about the end times.

Beyond its religious meaning, the Testament of Adam is part of a larger tradition of Jewish and Christian mystical writings, where history, divine messages, and the order of the universe are connected. It encourages readers to think about the patterns of worship and God's promises for the future. Whether seen as a prayerful text, an apocalyptic message, or an early Christian testimony, the Testament of Adam offers a deep reflection on humanity's role in God's plan.

By discussing the sacred hours, the prophecy of Christ, and the future of the world, this text connects the ancient past with the distant future. It serves as a reminder of the hope of salvation and the power of God over all things.

The Hours of The Day.

Understand this about the hours of the day and night, and how important it is to pray to God at the right times. My Creator taught me these things. He showed me the names of all the animals, the birds in the sky, and how each hour has a special meaning. He also revealed to me how the angels give praise to God.

Listen, my child, and know this:

- At the first hour of the day, my children's prayers rise up to God.
- At the second hour, the angels lift their prayers and requests to Him.
- At the third hour, the birds in the sky sing His praises.
- At the fourth hour, the spiritual beings worship Him.
- At the fifth hour, all the animals and wild creatures honor Him.
- At the sixth hour, the Cherubim make their petitions to Him.
- At the seventh hour, all the angels come before God and then leave His presence. At this time, every living thing's prayer reaches Him.
- At the eighth hour, the bright heavenly beings praise Him.

- At the ninth hour, the angels who stand before God's throne give Him honor.
- At the tenth hour, the Holy Spirit touches the waters, making the evil spirits flee. If the Holy Spirit did not bless the waters at this time each day, no one would be able to drink from them because evil spirits would make the water harmful. But if a priest takes water at this hour, mixes it with holy oil, and anoints the sick or those troubled by evil spirits, they will be healed.
- At the eleventh hour, the righteous people give their praises to God.
- At the twelfth hour, God listens to the prayers and requests of all people.

The Hours of The Night.

- At the first hour of the night, even the demons give thanks and praise to God Most High. During this time, they do not cause harm or trouble until they finish their worship.
- At the second hour, the fish and all sea creatures, including the great whales, lift their praises to God.
- At the third hour, fire itself gives praise. During this time, the fire is in the deepest parts of the earth, and no one can speak to God.
- At the fourth hour, the Seraphim (heavenly beings) declare God's holiness.
- At the fifth hour, the waters above the heavens give praise. Long ago, I listened to the angels at this hour and was amazed by the sound of their voices. They cried out like a powerful wheel turning, and their voices roared like ocean waves as they praised God.
- At the sixth hour, the clouds praise God with fear and trembling.
- At the seventh hour, everything on earth becomes still. The land and all creatures grow silent, and even the waters rest. If a

priest takes water at this time, mixes it with holy oil, and anoints the sick or those struggling to sleep, the sick will be healed, and the restless will find sleep.

- At the eighth hour, the earth brings forth grass, plants, and trees, causing them to grow leaves and fruit.
- At the ninth hour, the angels continue their worship, and the prayers of people rise up to God Most High.
- At the tenth hour, the gates of heaven open, and God listens to the prayers of believers. He answers the requests of those who call upon Him. At this moment, when the Seraphim spread their wings, the roosters crow and praise God.
- At the eleventh hour, joy spreads across the earth as the sun enters Paradise. Its light reaches all corners of the world, shining on everything that exists.
- At the twelfth hour, my children should stand before God and honor Him. At this time, a great silence falls over the heavens as all creation shows reverence.

Adam Foretells the Coming of Christ.

Now, listen carefully and understand this: The Word of God, the Most High, will come down to earth just as He told me when He sent me out of the Garden of Paradise. He said that in the future, His Word would become human, born from a virgin named Mary. He would take on flesh and be born as a man with great power, wisdom, and skill. Only He and those to whom He chooses to reveal Himself will truly know Him.

God told me that He would walk among people, grow older over the years, and perform many miracles. He would walk on water as if it were solid ground, command the sea and the wind, and they would obey Him. He would heal the blind, cleanse those with leprosy, make the deaf hear, and allow the mute to speak. He would heal those who were paralyzed, help the lame walk, lead many people away from false beliefs to the knowledge of God, and cast out demons from those who were possessed.

God also spoke to me and said, "Do not be sad, Adam. You wanted to become like a god and broke my command. I will restore you, but not now—it will happen in time." Then He said, "I am God, and I sent you out from the Garden of Joy into this world, where the ground will grow thorns and weeds. You will live here, your back will bend with age, your knees will grow weak, and your body will return to the earth to be eaten by worms. But after five and a half days, I will have mercy on you. I will come into your home, take on human flesh, and be born as a child. I will live among people, walk in the marketplace, fast for forty days, be baptized, suffer, and die on the cross—all of this I will do for you, Adam."

May He be praised, honored, and glorified forever and ever, along with His Father and the Holy Spirit. Amen.

And know this, my son Seth: A great flood will come and wash over the whole earth because of the wickedness of Cain's children. Cain, the murderer, killed his brother out of jealousy over their sister, Lud. After the flood, many years will pass, and the last days will come. Everything will be completed, and the time of judgment will arrive. Fire will consume everything before God, and the earth will be made holy again. Then, the Lord of Lords will walk upon it.

Seth wrote down this message and sealed it with his own seal, along with the seals of his father, Adam, and his mother, Eve—seals that had been taken from the Garden of Paradise.

Testament of Abraham

Abraham lived an incredibly long life, reaching 995 years. Throughout his years, he was known for his kindness, humility, and strong faith. He was also incredibly generous, always welcoming travelers at his tent near the oak of Mamre. It didn't matter who they were—rich or poor, powerful or weak, friends or strangers—Abraham treated everyone with the same kindness and respect. He was admired for his goodness, holiness, and hospitality.

But even for Abraham, the end of life had to come, just as it does for everyone. God, the ruler of all, called His archangel Michael and gave him an important task. "Michael, go to Abraham and tell him that his time on earth is coming to an end. Let him prepare to pass on his belongings. I have blessed him with countless descendants, as many as the stars in the sky and the grains of sand by the sea. He has lived a life full of wealth and prosperity, but more importantly, he has been righteous and kind until the very end. Now, it is time for him to leave this world and join Me among the righteous."

Michael obeyed God's command and descended to earth, finding Abraham near the oak of Mamre. Abraham was in the fields, watching over the plowing with the sons of Masek and twelve other workers. The archangel appeared in the form of a handsome soldier, and when Abraham saw him from a distance, he immediately stood up to greet him, as he always did with visitors.

Abraham welcomed him warmly, saying, "Greetings, noble soldier! You shine like the sun, and your beauty is greater than any man's. Welcome to my home. Please tell me, where have you come from, and who is your master?" The angel replied, "Abraham, I come from the great city of my King. He has sent me with a message. My King wishes to call His faithful friend to Him."

Abraham invited him to walk with him to his field. As they walked together, he told his servants, "Bring us two gentle and well-trained horses to ride." But Michael refused, saying, "No, my lord Abraham. I do not ride animals, for my King, who rules over all things, does not require such things for His messengers. Let us walk together with joy."

As they continued on, a tall cypress tree by the roadside suddenly spoke in a human voice, saying, "Holy, holy, holy is the Lord God, who calls His beloved to Himself." Abraham was shocked but tried to pretend he hadn't heard, thinking perhaps the angel had not noticed either.

When they reached the house, they sat in the courtyard. Isaac, Abraham's son, noticed the angel's glowing face and immediately ran to his mother, Sarah. "Mother, the man with Father is no ordinary person," he said. Then Isaac approached and bowed deeply before Michael. The angel blessed him, saying, "The Lord will keep His promise to you and your father Abraham. His blessings will be upon you."

Abraham, always eager to be a good host, told Isaac, "Bring water from the well so we may wash our guest's feet." Isaac quickly brought the water, and Abraham gently washed Michael's feet. As he did so, he became overwhelmed with emotion, and tears filled his eyes. Seeing his father cry, Isaac also began to weep. Moved by their kindness and sincerity, the angel Michael shed tears as well. His tears fell into the water, and when they touched the ground, the stones in the basin transformed into precious gems, sparkling with divine beauty.

Abraham watched in amazement but kept the event a secret in his heart. Quietly, he gathered the shining stones and hid them, understanding that they carried a deep and special meaning.

Turning to Isaac, Abraham spoke with love, "My son, prepare the guest room for our honored visitor. Make it beautiful—set up two couches, one for me and one for our guest. Arrange a table with plenty of food, and place a lampstand nearby. Lay soft linens, purple cloth, and fine silk on the floor. Burn the finest incense and bring fresh flowers and fragrant plants from the garden. Fill the house with their sweet scent. Light seven lamps with the purest oil, for this guest is more important than any king. Even his face shines brighter than all men."

Isaac obeyed his father's instructions carefully, making sure everything was just right. Meanwhile, Abraham led the angel Michael to the guest room. They entered together and sat down on the couches. Abraham placed a table in front of them, filled with a rich variety of food and drink.

After sitting for a while, the archangel Michael stood up and stepped outside, pretending he needed to take care of something. But in an instant, he rose into the sky and returned to the presence of God. Bowing before the Lord, Michael said, "Master, I cannot bring myself to tell Abraham that he is about to die. I have never met anyone as kind, generous, and faithful as he is. He truly fears You and avoids all evil. How can I give him such news?"

God, in His wisdom, answered, "Michael, My most trusted servant, go back to Abraham and do whatever he asks of you. Eat at his table, and I will send My Holy Spirit upon his son, Isaac. In a dream, Isaac will receive the knowledge of his father's approaching death. When he wakes, you will explain the dream to him, and through him, Abraham will understand what is coming."

Michael replied, "Lord, the heavenly beings do not have physical bodies. We do not eat or drink, yet Abraham has prepared a feast filled with earthly food. What should I do, Lord, so that I do not reveal my true nature while sitting at his table? How can I carry out Your will without making him suspicious?"

God, knowing Michael's concern, had already prepared a way for everything to unfold as planned. Abraham's incredible kindness and deep faith had touched even the heavens, making way for an important revelation.

Later, Isaac experienced a strange and unsettling vision. At first, he stood peacefully under the light of the sun and moon. But suddenly, their light faded, and they began to drift away from him. Darkness surrounded him, and a cold fear filled his heart. Then, from the distance, he saw a glowing figure, shining brighter than the sun. The figure held a sickle and had a solemn yet sorrowful expression. As he drew closer, Isaac felt an overwhelming sense that this being had come for someone dear to him.

The figure stopped in front of him and spoke in a voice that was both powerful and gentle. "The time has come for the righteous to enter eternal rest. Do not be afraid. The one I seek has lived a faithful life and will be welcomed with great joy."

Isaac's heart sank. He knew the figure was speaking about his father, Abraham. He tried to reach out, but the being disappeared, and he woke up shaking and in tears. He immediately ran to his father and said, "Father, I had a terrible dream, and I fear it means I will lose you."

When Abraham heard Isaac's vision, he felt both sorrow and a deep sense of awe. He turned to Michael and asked, "Tell me, noble guest, does this dream reveal what is to come? Speak the truth, for I can feel that God's hand is at work in all of this."

With a kind but serious voice, Michael answered, "Abraham, beloved of God, your son's dream was not just a vision—it was a message from the Lord. The time has come for you to leave this world and enter God's eternal presence. You have lived a life of faith, kindness, and righteousness, and a place has been prepared for you among the chosen ones. Do not fear, for your legacy will live on through your children, and the promises made to you will be fulfilled."

Hearing this, Sarah, who had been listening from the doorway, began to cry. She entered the room, wrapped her arms around Abraham, and said, "My love, if this is truly God's will, then who are we to resist it? But my heart aches at the thought of losing you. Please promise me that even after you leave, you will pray for us as you rest in the presence of the Lord."

Abraham gently comforted her, saying, "Do not weep, my dear wife. Though I will no longer be here in body, I will be closer to God and will continue to pray for you and our children. Let us trust in His plan, for He is always faithful and merciful."

He then turned to Isaac, placed his hands on his son's head, and blessed him. "My son, you are the light of my old age, the proof of God's promise. Walk in His ways, seek justice, and show mercy to others. Through you and your descendants, all nations will be blessed."

Isaac, though filled with sorrow, nodded with determination. He would honor his father's legacy.

Then Abraham looked at Michael and said, "Tell the Lord that His servant is ready. May His will be done."

Michael bowed in respect and said, "Your faith will be remembered for all generations, Abraham. The heavens rejoice because of your steadfastness, and your name will never be forgotten."

The family came together in prayer, lifting their voices in praise and gratitude, even as they prepared for their final moments with Abraham. Everyone in the household treated this time with deep reverence, knowing that their beloved patriarch was about to be welcomed into eternity.

Then, another vision appeared before Isaac's eyes. He saw the heavens open, revealing a breathtaking sight. A figure, shining with a brilliance greater than seven suns combined, descended from above. This radiant being approached Isaac and carefully lifted the sun from his head, carrying it back into the heavens. As the sun disappeared, a deep sadness filled Isaac's heart, and he grieved its loss.

As he continued to mourn, the radiant figure returned and took the moon from him as well. Overcome with sorrow, Isaac cried out, "No, my lord! Do not take both my sun and moon! Please, have mercy! If you must take the sun, at least leave me the moon!"

The glowing figure spoke with both authority and kindness. "They must be taken to the King above, for He desires them there." Though Isaac pleaded, the being carried both the sun and moon away. However, their light remained behind, a sign that their presence would never truly be gone.

Michael, standing nearby, explained, "Listen closely, Isaac. In your vision, the sun represents your father, Abraham, and the moon represents your mother, Sarah. The radiant figure was a messenger from God, sent to bring your father's soul into the presence of the Almighty. It is now time for Abraham to leave the earthly world and enter God's eternal kingdom."

When Abraham heard this, he turned to Michael and said, "This is truly an amazing and powerful revelation! Are you the one who will take my soul from me?"

Michael answered seriously, "I am Michael, the leader of the heavenly armies, and I stand before the Lord. I was sent here to tell you that your time on earth is ending, as God has commanded. Once my task is complete, I will return to Him."

Abraham, realizing that Michael was truly a messenger from God, replied firmly, "Now I understand that you are an angel of the Lord, sent to take my soul. But I must tell you this—I will not willingly go with you. You must do as you are commanded, but I will not follow."

Hearing Abraham's response, Michael disappeared and returned to heaven. Standing before God's throne, he reported everything that had happened at Abraham's house. He told the Lord, "Your friend Abraham has said, 'I will not follow you, no matter what. Do what you have been ordered to do.' Almighty Lord, what do You command now?"

God, in His wisdom, answered Michael, "Return to My beloved Abraham and tell him this: 'I am the Lord your God. I brought you into the promised land and blessed you beyond measure. I made your descendants as countless as the stars in the sky and the sand on the shore. I opened Sarah's barren womb and gave you Isaac, the son I promised. I have answered all your prayers and given you everything you have asked for.

So tell Me, Abraham, why do you resist Me now? Why is your heart troubled, and why have you refused My messenger Michael? Do you not understand that all people born from Adam and Eve must experience death? No prophet has escaped it, and no king has ruled forever without facing it. Every ancestor before you, no matter how righteous, has passed through the mystery of death.

But you, Abraham, have been shown great mercy. I did not send Death to take you as I have done with others. I protected you from sickness and from falling into the hands of the grave. I have spared you from the suffering that others go through at the end of life. Instead, I sent My most trusted messenger, Michael, to warn you gently, so you could prepare your household, bless your son Isaac, and set your affairs in order. I did this not to trouble you, but to honor you. So why have you resisted My messenger and said, 'I will not go'? Do you not realize that if I allowed Death to come for you, you would have no choice? Think about this, My beloved servant.'"

With these words, Michael prepared to return to Abraham, carrying God's message of authority and compassion.

Michael obeyed and once again descended to Abraham. When Abraham saw Michael approaching, his strength left him, and he collapsed to the ground, trembling as if lifeless. The angel gently spoke to him, repeating every word that God had said.

Upon hearing this, Abraham stood up, but tears ran down his face. Overcome with emotion, he fell at Michael's feet and pleaded, "Mighty leader of the heavenly armies, you have come to me, a mere human, with great kindness. But I have one more request. Please take my words back to the Lord, the Master of all things. Tell Him, 'Lord, my God, You have always heard my prayers and answered me with grace. Every request I have ever made, You have fulfilled.

Now, my Lord, I do not refuse Your will. I know that I am only human and not immortal. I understand that my life on earth must end, and I know that all things tremble before Your power. But I ask You for just one more thing before I go. While my spirit is still in my body, let me see the fullness of the world You created—the vast earth, the wonders You made with a single word. Let me witness these marvels, and then, when the time comes for me to leave, I will go in peace, without sorrow or regret.'"

Michael listened to Abraham's request and then returned to God's throne to deliver the message. Bowing before the Almighty, he said, "Lord Most High, Your faithful servant Abraham humbly asks for this: 'Allow me to see the whole world before I leave this life, so I may admire Your creation and go in peace.'"

God, hearing the words of His beloved friend, responded with both compassion and authority. "Michael, My Commander, take a cloud of light and summon the angels who guide the heavenly chariots. Go to My servant Abraham and lift him onto a chariot of cherubim. Carry him up into the heavens so he may see all of the earth and the works of My hands."

Michael followed the Lord's command and returned to Abraham. With the help of sixty angels, he lifted Abraham onto a bright chariot of cherubim. They rose into the air, surrounded by a cloud of divine light. From this height, Abraham was able to see the entire world just as it was on that day.

He saw people going about their daily lives—some plowing fields, others guiding wagons, tending sheep, or working in the countryside. In some places, people were celebrating, dancing, playing music, or wrestling for sport. In other areas, legal disputes were being settled, judges made decisions, and mourners wept as they carried their dead to burial. He also saw joyful wedding processions, celebrating the union of husband and wife.

As he observed the world, Abraham saw both good and evil. Some people were performing righteous acts, while others were lost in wrongdoing. As the chariot continued its journey, he noticed a group of men carrying sharp swords, preparing for violence and destruction. Troubled by their wickedness, he turned to Michael and asked, "Who are these men, and what are they planning?"

Michael replied, "They are robbers, planning to kill, steal, and destroy."

Filled with righteous anger, Abraham cried out to the Lord, "Lord, hear my prayer! Send wild beasts from the forests to destroy these evildoers!"

As soon as he spoke, wild animals emerged from the trees and attacked the wicked men, tearing them apart.

As the journey continued, Abraham saw a man and a woman committing shameful acts in public. Shocked, he called out, "Lord, please command the earth to open up and swallow them so they no longer corrupt the world with their sins." Immediately, the ground beneath them split apart, and they were pulled into the earth's depths.

Moving forward, Abraham came across another troubling scene. He saw men breaking into a house, stealing things that didn't belong to them. Deeply disturbed, he prayed, "Lord, send down fire from heaven to destroy these thieves!" In response, fire rained down from the sky and consumed them.

As Abraham watched fire descend and destroy the wrongdoers, a powerful voice from heaven spoke directly to Michael. It carried the authority of the Most High and commanded, "Michael, stop the chariot and turn Abraham away from these sights. If he continues to witness the sins of the world, he will destroy everything. Abraham is righteous, but he has no mercy on those who sin. Yet I, the Creator of all things, do not seek to destroy the world. I do not wish for sinners to die but to have time to change their ways and be saved. Now, take Abraham to the first gate of heaven so he may witness judgment. Let him see what happens to the souls he has condemned, and may he learn to show mercy."

Michael obeyed God's command and directed the chariot eastward, bringing Abraham to the first gate of heaven. When they arrived, Abraham saw two different paths. One was narrow and difficult, while the other was wide and easy. These paths led to two gates—the narrow path connected to the small gate, and the broad path led to a large, open gate.

Near these gates, Abraham saw a man sitting on a golden throne. His presence was overwhelming, both awe-inspiring and intimidating, almost like that of the Lord Himself. Abraham watched as countless souls were led by angels through the broad gate, while only a few entered through the narrow one.

The man on the throne reacted intensely to what he saw. When only a few souls entered the narrow gate, he pulled at his hair and beard, collapsed to the ground, and wept bitterly. But when he saw some souls making it through the narrow gate, his entire expression changed. He stood up, returned to his throne, and rejoiced, his face glowing with happiness.

Curious, Abraham turned to Michael and asked, "Who is this man, sitting in such splendor, who grieves one moment and celebrates the next?"

Michael explained, "This is Adam, the first man, and the father of all humanity. He is honored because all people came from him. When he sees souls entering the narrow gate that leads to life and Paradise, he rejoices because these souls are saved. But when he watches countless souls enter the broad gate that leads to destruction, he is overwhelmed with sorrow. He throws himself to the ground and cries because he mourns for his lost descendants. So many are lost, and so few are saved. Out of seven thousand souls, barely one is found to be pure and righteous."

As Michael spoke, Abraham saw something terrifying. Two angels appeared, their bodies covered in flames, their faces stern and unyielding. They drove a huge crowd of souls before them, striking them with fiery whips. One angel tightly gripped a single soul, while the other led many toward the broad gate of destruction.

Abraham and Michael followed them through the broad gate and entered a place of judgment. Inside, Abraham saw a throne that seemed to be made of blazing crystal. Its brightness was beyond anything he had ever seen. Sitting on the throne was a figure shining like the sun, looking like a divine son of God.

Before the throne stood a large golden table covered with fine linen. On the table rested a massive book, six cubits thick and ten cubits wide. Beside the table stood two angels, one on each side, holding pens and scrolls, ready to write down the deeds of souls. In front of the table, a glowing angel held a scale, while another fiery angel stood nearby, his expression fierce and unrelenting.

This fiery angel carried a trumpet filled with consuming flames, which he used to test the souls of the condemned.

The glowing figure on the throne served as the judge, deciding the fate of each soul brought before him. The angels standing on either side carefully recorded every person's actions—good deeds on the right and sins on the left. Another angel weighed each soul on a scale, while the fiery angel tested them with flames.

Watching this, Abraham turned to Michael and asked, "What does all of this mean?"

Michael replied, "These are the judgments of the Most High. Here, every soul is measured, and each one receives the outcome it deserves."

As they watched, one of the fiery angels led a soul forward and presented it to the judge. The judge then ordered an angel to open the great book and find the soul's record. Abraham stood in silence, feeling the weight of what was happening before him.

The angel turned the pages of the book, carefully reviewing the soul's deeds. It was discovered that its good and bad actions were perfectly balanced. Because of this, the soul was not sent to suffer punishment, nor was it welcomed among the saved. Instead, it was placed in an in-between state, neither condemned nor fully redeemed.

Abraham, deeply affected by what he saw, turned to Michael and asked, "My lord, who is this powerful judge who decides the fate of souls? Who are the angels keeping records? Who holds the scale, and who is the angel of fire?"

With great respect, Michael answered, "Righteous Abraham, do you see the mighty figure seated on the throne? That is Abel, the son of Adam, the first man. Abel was righteous, but he was murdered by his brother Cain. Because of this, God appointed him as the judge of humanity, saying, 'I will not judge people directly; instead, they will be judged by one of their own.' Abel remains the judge of souls until the day when the Lord Himself comes to bring the final judgment. On that day, all justice will be carried out perfectly and without question.

"This judgment you see now is the first of three. The second will take place during the Lord's return, when the twelve tribes of Israel will judge all souls and creatures. The third and final judgment will be carried out by God Himself. That will be the ultimate verdict—final and unchangeable. The world is judged thoroughly, with three witnesses, just as it is written: 'Every matter must be confirmed by the testimony of three witnesses.'

"The two angels beside the throne record every person's actions. The angel on the right writes down good deeds, while the angel on the left records sins. The bright angel holding the scale is Dokiel, the archangel responsible for measuring deeds according to God's justice.

The fierce, fiery angel holding the flames is Purouel, who has been given control over fire. He tests every person's deeds. If the fire burns away all their actions, that soul is immediately taken to the place of suffering. But if their deeds remain unharmed, they are declared righteous and are taken to join the saved. This is how every soul is tested—by fire and by balance—to reveal the truth of their life."

Abraham, still thinking about the soul that was left in the middle, asked, "Commander Michael, why was this soul placed between the two fates? What does it mean?"

Michael explained, "This soul's good and bad deeds were equal. Because of that, it was neither condemned nor saved. It must wait here until the final Judge arrives to make the last decision."

Abraham, filled with compassion, asked, "What would allow this soul to be saved? What is still needed for it to be redeemed?"

Michael replied, "If this soul could gain even one more good deed than its sins, the balance would shift in its favor, and it would be saved."

Overcome with a sense of urgency and mercy, Abraham said, "Michael, let us pray together for this soul. Perhaps the Lord will hear us and grant it a chance to be saved."

Michael, respecting Abraham's request, prepared to join him in prayer, knowing the depth of Abraham's faith and the great mercy of the Most High.

As Michael and Abraham prayed with all their hearts for the soul, Abraham said sincerely, "Amen, let it be so." Together, they called out to God, pleading for His mercy and grace. Their prayers were filled with deep emotion, and God heard them.

When they finished praying, Abraham turned to Michael and asked, "Where is the soul that was here in the middle?"

Michael smiled gently and said, "Because of your righteous prayer, Abraham, the soul has been saved. A light-filled angel has taken it to Paradise."

Overcome with gratitude, Abraham raised his hands toward heaven and praised God. "I give glory to the Most High and His endless mercy!"

But even after this, Abraham still felt uneasy. He turned back to Michael and said, "Archangel, please hear my request once more. Let us humble ourselves before the Lord again and ask for His mercy. I want to pray for the souls of the sinners I condemned. The ones swallowed by the earth, torn apart by wild animals, or burned by fire— all because of my words. Now I understand that I was wrong. I see that I sinned against the Lord. Michael, great leader of heaven's armies, I beg you to join me in asking for forgiveness. Let us cry out to the Lord with humble hearts and ask Him to forgive me and bring those souls back to life."

Michael saw the sincerity of Abraham's repentance and nodded solemnly. "Let it be so."

Together, they knelt and prayed with deep sorrow, their voices filled with regret and hope. They cried out for God's mercy, asking for the restoration of those who had been judged. After a long time, a powerful voice echoed from heaven, strong and full of majesty:

"Abraham, Abraham, I have heard your prayer. I forgive your sin. The people you believed were destroyed, I have restored and brought back to life through My great kindness. I punished them for a time, but I do not hold eternal anger against those who live on the earth. My desire is not destruction, but that people turn away from their sins and be made whole again."

Then the voice spoke to Michael, saying, "Michael, My faithful servant, return Abraham to his home. His time on earth is almost over, and the days of his life are complete. He must prepare his household, settle his affairs, and then come to Me."

Following this command, Michael guided the heavenly chariot and cloud back to Abraham's home. When they arrived, Abraham entered his room and sat on his couch, his heart heavy with the weight of all he had experienced.

Sarah, his beloved wife, saw him return and immediately ran to him, falling at his feet in tears. "My love, I thank God that you have come back to me! We feared you had been taken from us."

Soon after, their son Isaac came running, throwing his arms around his father's neck with relief and joy. All of Abraham's servants, both men and women, gathered around him, surrounding him with love and gratitude, praising God for his safe return.

Michael then spoke with kindness but also authority. "Listen to me, righteous Abraham. Look at your wife Sarah, your son Isaac, and all those who love you. The time has come to set your house in order, for soon you will leave this world and return to the presence of the Lord."

Abraham felt sorrow at these words and asked, "Is this truly the Lord's command, or do you say this on your own?"

Michael answered with deep respect, "Righteous Abraham, these are the words of the Lord. He has sent me to tell you."

Even after hearing this, Abraham stood firm and replied, "I will not go with you."

When Michael heard Abraham's response, he left and returned to heaven. Standing before God, he reported everything that had happened. "Lord Almighty, I have fulfilled every request of Your servant Abraham. I have shown him Your power, the earth, the sea, and the judgment of souls. But once again, he has refused, saying, 'I will not follow you.'"

God, with great patience, asked, "Does My friend Abraham still refuse to go with you?"

Michael replied, "Yes, Lord. These were his words. But I have not forced him, for he has always been faithful to You, pleasing You in all he does. No one on earth, not even Job, compares to him in righteousness. I now await Your command, O eternal King."

The Lord then commanded, "Call Death, the one with the dreadful appearance and merciless power."

Michael obeyed and summoned Death, who appeared before God, trembling and groaning under the weight of divine authority. The Lord spoke to him, saying, "Hide your fearsome form and the stench of decay. Remove your harshness and take on a youthful, beautiful appearance. Dress yourself in glory and radiance. Go to My friend Abraham and take him gently. Speak to him with kindness and respect, for he is dear to Me."

Death transformed into a being of breathtaking beauty, brighter than any human, dressed in dazzling robes. With divine light surrounding him, he set off to meet Abraham.

At that moment, Abraham had stepped outside and was sitting under the shade of the trees at Mamre. He rested his chin on his hand, lost in thought, waiting for Michael to return. Suddenly, a sweet fragrance filled the air, carried by a brilliant light unlike anything he had ever seen. Turning toward the presence, Abraham saw a magnificent figure approaching, glowing with youthful beauty and dressed in splendor. Thinking it was Michael, the leader of God's angels, Abraham stood to greet him.

As Death approached, he knelt respectfully before Abraham and spoke with deep reverence. "Greetings, righteous Abraham, faithful servant of the Most High, and companion of the holy angels."

Abraham, amazed by his appearance, replied, "Greetings, radiant one. You shine like the sun, more beautiful than any man. You carry the light of heaven itself. Tell me, who are you, and where have you come from?"

With a solemn tone, Death answered, "Righteous Abraham, I am the bitter cup of death."

Abraham, surprised, shook his head. "No, that cannot be true. You are too beautiful, full of light and goodness. You do not look bitter or dreadful. How can you say you are Death?"

Death calmly replied, "Abraham, I am what the Most High has named me to be. This is my purpose."

Abraham's expression grew serious. "Then why have you come here?"

Death answered plainly, "I have come to take your soul."

Now fully understanding, Abraham firmly said, "I hear your words, but I will not follow you." Death did not respond but remained silent.

Abraham turned and walked back into his house, but Death followed closely behind. Entering his room, Abraham climbed onto his couch, seeking rest. However, Death sat down at the foot of the couch, refusing to leave.

Annoyed by his presence, Abraham said, "Go away! I want to rest."

But Death replied, "I will not leave until I have taken your soul with me."

Abraham's eyes narrowed. "By the immortal God, I command you to tell me the truth. Are you really Death?"

With a heavy voice, Death answered, "Yes, I am Death, the one who brings an end to all life on earth."

Abraham, now curious, asked, "Tell me, do you always appear like this—so full of beauty, youth, and light?"

Death softened his voice. "No, righteous Abraham. To those like you, I come in beauty, bringing peace and gentleness. But to sinners, I appear as a terrifying and merciless figure, filled with decay and horror."

Abraham's eyes flashed with determination. "Then show me this dreadful form you speak of. Let me see your true appearance."

Death hesitated before responding. "You would not be able to bear the sight of my true form, Abraham. Even the strongest souls would tremble before my full presence."

But Abraham stood firm. "By the name of the living God, I will endure it. The power of my God is with me, and I will not be afraid."

Giving in to Abraham's request, Death let go of his beautiful, glowing appearance. The bright, sun-like form he had taken disappeared, revealing his true, terrifying nature. His face darkened, becoming more dreadful than the fiercest beasts, and his body reeked of filth and decay.

Death then revealed seven fiery dragon heads and fourteen terrifying faces. One was engulfed in flames, another was pitch black and shadowy, one looked like a venomous snake, and another was jagged and sharp like a steep cliff. One was more menacing than a deadly serpent, another had the face of a roaring lion, and one resembled a monstrous horned cobra. He also showed a face that glowed like a burning sword, another that thundered with deafening noise, and one that churned like a raging sea and violent river. Finally, Death revealed a monstrous three-headed dragon, a cup filled with deadly poison, and every imaginable image of destruction and terror, all carrying the stench of death itself.

The sight was so horrifying that it sent shockwaves through Abraham's entire household. Every servant—about seven thousand men and women—collapsed in fear and died instantly. Even Abraham himself felt the overwhelming presence of death pressing down on him, and his spirit began to weaken.

Overcome by the terrifying vision, Abraham turned to Death and pleaded, "I beg you, merciless destroyer, hide this dreadful form of yours and return to the youthful beauty and light you showed before."

Hearing Abraham's plea, Death immediately shed his monstrous appearance and returned to the glorious, radiant form he had worn earlier.

Still shaken, Abraham asked, "Why did you do this? You have caused the death of all my servants! Was this the reason God sent you to me today?"

Death responded calmly, "No, righteous Abraham. I was not sent here for them—I came for you."

Abraham's heart grew heavier. "Then why did they die? Surely the Lord did not command this."

Death explained, "Believe me, righteous Abraham, it is a miracle that you yourself were not taken with them. If not for the protection of God's right hand, you too would have perished in that moment. Only His mercy has kept you here."

Hearing these words, Abraham felt the weight of what had happened. "Now I understand that I had stepped into the shadow of death, and my spirit nearly failed. But I ask you, Death, since my servants have died too soon because of your terrifying presence, let us pray together before the Lord our God. Let us ask Him to bring them back to life."

Death agreed, saying, "Amen, let it be so."

Abraham fell face down on the ground in deep prayer, and Death knelt beside him in supplication. God, moved by their prayer, sent forth His spirit of life, and all the servants who had died were revived. Seeing this great miracle, Abraham lifted his hands in praise and glorified God for His endless mercy and kindness.

After this, Abraham went up to his room to rest, but Death followed him and stood beside his bed. Abraham, exhausted, turned to him and said, "Leave me now. I need to rest. My spirit is weighed down with sorrow."

But Death replied, "I will not leave until I have taken your soul."

Abraham, his face stern and his eyes filled with strength, responded, "Who told you to speak like this? Your words are arrogant, and I will not follow you. Not until Michael, the Commander of Heaven's armies, comes for me. Only then will I go. But if you want me to listen to you, then first, answer my questions. Explain to me the meaning of the visions I saw—why did you appear with seven fiery dragon heads, the face of a cliff, a sharp sword, a raging river, a stormy sea, thunder, lightning, and a cup of deadly poison? Tell me what they represent."

Death, seeing how determined Abraham was, spoke to him and said, "Listen, righteous Abraham. For many ages, I have traveled across the world, bringing all people—kings and rulers, the rich and the poor, the free and the enslaved—down to the grave. No one escapes my grasp. That is why I showed you the seven dragon heads. Each one represents the different ways I bring death into the world.

"I showed you the face of fire because many die in flames. Fire burns them up, and they experience death in its heat. The face of the cliff represents those who fall from great heights—whether from trees, mountains, or buildings. As they fall, they face death. The face of the sword symbolizes all those who die in battle, struck down by blades, meeting death in its sharp edge.

"The face of the raging river stands for those who are drowned, either in great floods or strong currents. They are swept away and struggle to breathe before they die. The stormy sea's face represents those lost in shipwrecks, swallowed by the waves, seeing death in the depths of the ocean.

"The loud thunder and deadly lightning I showed you represent those struck down by storms. When lightning flashes and thunder roars, many die in fear.

"The wild beasts—the snakes, leopards, lions, and vipers—represent those who are killed by animals, either torn apart or poisoned by their venom. Many die in pain and terror from these attacks.

"The cup of poison stands for those who are betrayed by others and given deadly drinks. The poison spreads through their bodies, killing them unexpectedly."

As Abraham listened to Death explain these terrifying truths, he realized how vast and inescapable death truly was. He sat in deep thought, shaken by what he had learned.

With a trembling voice, Abraham asked Death, "Tell me, is it true that some people die suddenly, without any warning? I wish to understand."

Death answered, "Yes, righteous Abraham. I swear to you, with the truth of God, that there are seventy-two ways to die. Some people pass away at their appointed time, as expected, but many others die suddenly, without any warning. They are here one moment and gone the next. I have told you the truth as you asked. Now, Abraham, the time has come. Put aside your doubts and last wishes. It is time to fulfill the will of the One who rules all. Come with me, for the Master has commanded it."

Abraham, his voice weak, said, "Please, just a little more time. Let me rest for a while. My heart feels weak, and my body is growing heavy. Ever since I looked upon you, my strength has left me. My limbs feel as heavy as stone, and it is hard to breathe. Please, leave me for a little while. I cannot bear to see you any longer."

Abraham lay down, and soon his son Isaac entered, filled with grief. He threw himself onto his father's chest and wept bitterly. Not long after, Sarah, Abraham's wife, came in and fell at his feet, crying as tears streamed down her face. All of Abraham's servants gathered around, mourning loudly. The entire room was filled with sorrow, and as Abraham felt his life slipping away, he sank deeper into the darkness of death.

Then, in a calm and almost soothing voice, Death spoke again. "Come now, righteous one. Kiss my right hand, and I promise you will feel light, joyful, and full of life again." But Death was deceiving him. Trusting these words, Abraham kissed Death's hand, and at that moment, his soul left his body, drawn into Death's grasp.

At that instant, the archangel Michael appeared with a host of angels. They took Abraham's soul gently, wrapping it in shining heavenly cloths. They anointed his body with sacred oils and perfumes, preparing him with great care. For three days, the angels watched over Abraham, honoring him with deep respect.

On the third day, they carried his body to its final resting place in the promised land, near the great oak of Mamre. At the same time, the angels lifted Abraham's soul into the heavens, singing beautiful hymns as they brought him before the throne of God.

As the angels sang songs of praise, God's voice filled the heavens. With love and authority, He said, "Bring my faithful servant Abraham into Paradise, the place of rest I have prepared for those who are righteous. Take him to the home of the holy ones, where Isaac and Jacob dwell in peace. There, there is no suffering, no sorrow, no pain— only joy, celebration, and eternal life."

Let us, dear friends, strive to live with the kindness, faith, and righteousness of Abraham. If we follow his example, we too may be worthy of the eternal life that God has promised. Let us give glory to the Father, the Son, and the Holy Spirit, now and forever. Amen.

Testament of Isaac

Isaac, the old and wise patriarch, wrote down his final words and shared them with his son Jacob and everyone gathered around. These words weren't just for them, but for anyone in the future who might hear them. He called his message a set of life-giving instructions—like medicine for the soul. He prayed that God's kindness would be with all who believe. He reminded them that true faith means holding on to God's words and patiently living by them. Everyone who believes in what God and His holy ones have said will become part of His kingdom. God was with the faithful before, and He will be with the faithful in the future too.

When Isaac's life was coming to an end, God sent the angel who had served his father Abraham. It was early in the morning on the twenty-second day of the month of Mesore. The angel greeted him and said, "Hello, son of promise!" Isaac, who often spoke with angels, looked up and saw that the angel looked just like his father. Filled with joy, he shouted, "Seeing your face feels like seeing the face of God!"

The angel said, "Isaac, I've come to take you to heaven, where your father Abraham is waiting for you. A throne has been prepared next to his. You and your son Jacob have been given a special place—greater than anyone else in creation. That's why you are called the Patriarch and the Father of the World."

Isaac, surprised, said, "You look just like my father."

The angel replied, "I serve your father Abraham. But now I've come to take you from sorrow into joy, from pain into peace. I will lead you from this world to a place of light, happiness, and freedom. Write your will, give your final words to your family, because I am taking you to eternal rest. Your father is blessed for raising you. You are blessed. Your son Jacob is blessed. And your descendants will be blessed too."

Jacob had heard some of the conversation but kept silent. Isaac, feeling sorrowful, asked, "What will happen to Jacob, the light of my life? I worry that Esau may harm him—you know the situation."

The angel replied, "Isaac, even if all the nations of the world tried, they could never take away the blessing you gave Jacob. When you blessed him, the Father, the Son, and the Holy Spirit also blessed him. Michael, Gabriel, all the angels, all the holy ones, and your father Abraham said 'Amen.' No weapon will harm him. He will be honored, become strong, and father twelve tribes."

Isaac said, "That gives me peace. But please don't tell Jacob, so he doesn't become upset."

The angel said, "Isaac, every faithful person is blessed when they leave this world and meet God. But those who live in sin—how terrible it will be for them. That's why you must pass these words down to your children. Tell Jacob everything your father told you. Then he can write them down and share them with future generations. Those who love God will live by these teachings. Be ready, so I can take you with joy. And now, I leave you with the same peace God gave me."

After saying this, the angel rose from the bed and returned to heaven. Isaac watched in amazement and whispered to himself, "I won't see another sunrise before I'm called."

Just then, Jacob walked into the room. Earlier, the angel had made him fall asleep so he wouldn't hear their talk. Now awake, he ran to his father and asked, "Father, who were you talking to?"

Isaac said, "You heard enough, my son. God has sent for me."

Jacob threw his arms around his father and wept. "Oh no! I've lost my strength. You're leaving me an orphan today."

Isaac hugged him tightly, and they cried together until they had no more tears left. Jacob begged, "Take me with you, Father."

Isaac replied, "No, my son. Wait for your time. I remember when the earth shook, and I spoke with your grandfather Abraham—I had no strength left. God's plan for each person is firm, and no one can change it. But I'm happy because I know I'm going to be with God. This is a path no one can avoid.

"Listen, my son—where are Adam and Eve, the first people God made? Where is Abel? Where are Mahalalel, Jared, Enoch, Methuselah, Noah, and his sons Shem, Ham, and Japheth? And after them— Arpachshad, Cainan, Shelah, Eber, Reu, Serug, Nahor, my father Terah, and his brother Lot? They all passed away—except for Enoch, who was taken up by God.

"After these, forty-two generations will pass until Christ is born from a pure virgin named Mary. He will live for thirty years and teach the world. Then He'll choose twelve men, show them sacred mysteries, and teach them about the meaning of His body and blood through bread and wine. The bread will become His body. The wine will become His blood.

"He will die on a cross for everyone. On the third day, He will rise again, defeat death, and save all people from evil. Everyone after that will be saved through His body and blood until the end of time. Christians will continue offering His sacrifice—whether in secret or in public. As long as they do, the Antichrist won't appear.

"Blessed is anyone who takes part in this sacred service and believes in it, because the real worship also happens in heaven. And one day, they will celebrate with the Son of God in His kingdom."

As Isaac spoke these words, his whole household gathered and cried. Jacob called their relatives, and they came in tears. Isaac had built a special room in his house where he lived once his eyesight failed. He had lived there for one hundred years, fasting each day until evening.

He offered animals to God for the souls of himself and his family. He spent half the night in prayer and praise. He lived a life of discipline and devotion for a full century. Every year, he fasted three times for forty days. He avoided wine, fruit, and even his own bed. He was always praying and thanking God.

Later, people heard that this holy man had regained his sight. Crowds came from all around to hear his wise words. They could tell God's Spirit was speaking through him. Even the most important guests asked him, "How is it that you can see again, after being blind for so long?"

The gentle old man smiled warmly and said, "My sons and brothers, the God of my father Abraham has done all this to bring me comfort in my old age." Then the priest stepped forward and asked, "Father Isaac, what should I do with my life?"

Isaac replied, "Keep your body pure, because your body is like a temple where God's presence lives. Don't get into arguments—you might say something you'll regret in anger. Watch what you say. Don't brag, don't gossip, and don't speak without thinking. Keep your hands from taking anything that isn't yours. When you offer a sacrifice to God, make sure it's clean and without flaws. Wash yourself with water before approaching the altar. Don't let worldly thoughts distract you while you're standing before God.

"Try to live peacefully with everyone. And when you give your offering, quietly say a hundred prayers to God and confess like this: 'God, You are beyond all understanding. Cleanse me with Your love. I am weak, and I have sinned. I come to You asking for Your mercy. I carry a heavy burden, and I ask You to take it away. Just as fire burns wood, let Your kindness burn away my sins. I ask for Your forgiveness. I forgive everyone You've created. I have no hate in my heart. I'm at peace with all people. I am Your servant, and You are the one who forgives. Please allow me to stand in Your holy place. Let my offering be accepted. Don't turn me away because of my sins. Welcome me like a lost sheep returning home. You were with Adam, Abel, Noah, Abraham, Isaac, and Jacob—please be with me too. Accept this sacrifice I bring to You.'

"As you say these things, offer your sacrifice with your heart focused on heaven. Don't treat this role lightly, because being a priest is a serious and sacred responsibility."

He went on, "Every priest, from now until the end of time, should live with self-control. That means watching what he eats, drinks, and how much he sleeps. He should stay away from worldly talk and not listen to gossip. Instead, he should fill his life with prayer, stay awake in worship, and read holy teachings, until God calls him home in peace.

"Whether a priest or a monk, anyone who chooses a holy life should turn away from the distractions of the world. They should live like the angels, who worship God in purity. Their sacrifices and devotion will be honored by God and the angels. The angels will even be their friends because of their strong faith and clean hearts.

"To sum it up, God expects us to avoid all sin—big or small. Here are the main sins we must repent from:

- Don't kill, whether with weapons or with cruel words.
- Don't sin with your body or your thoughts.
- Don't hurt young people.
- Don't be jealous.
- Don't stay angry past sunset.
- Don't be proud.
- Don't celebrate when someone else falls.
- Don't speak badly about others or listen to people who do.
- Don't look at others with lust in your eyes.

We have to be careful not to fall into these sins, or others like them, so we won't face the punishment that will come from heaven."

When everyone heard this, they cried out together, "Yes! This is true. Amen!" Isaac said no more. He pulled his blanket over his face, and everyone—both the people and the priest—grew quiet so he could rest.

Then the angel who had served his father Abraham came and took him up to heaven. There, Isaac saw terrifying things. He saw creatures with faces like camels, lions, and dogs. Some had just one eye. Some held long metal tongs made of iron.

He watched as a man was brought before these beasts. The ones guiding him stepped back. A lion came forward, tore him to pieces, and swallowed him. Then the beast vomited him up, and he became whole again. Another creature did the same—tearing, swallowing, and spitting him out. This went on as each beast took turns.

Isaac asked the angel, "What did this man do to deserve such horrible treatment?"

The angel answered, "This man had a fight with his neighbor and died without making peace. Now he's being punished by five main tormentors. For every hour he spent fighting, he suffers for an entire year."

The angel added, "Isaac, don't think this is unusual. There are 600,000 tormentors in total. If someone dies without repenting, they suffer a year of torment for every hour they spent sinning."

Then the angel took Isaac to a river of fire, waist-deep, roaring like thunder. He saw many souls trapped in it, crying and screaming. The fire burned only the guilty, not the innocent. The stench was terrible, and the wicked were boiled in it.

He also saw a deep, dark pit with smoke rising from it. People were stuck inside, grinding their teeth and groaning. The angel said, "Look over here too." Isaac saw more people suffering—those who had committed the worst sins, especially those from Sodom. Their pain was even greater.

He saw pits full of worms that never rested. He saw a fiery being named Abdemerouchos, in charge of the punishments. This being shouted at the tormentors, "Keep beating them until they understand that God is real!"

Isaac also saw a house made of fire. Grown men were trapped underneath it, crying out in pain. The angel said, "Look carefully at all this suffering. Let it stay with you."

Isaac said, "I can't take it. How long will these punishments last?"

The angel answered, "Until the merciful God decides to show them pity."

The angel took me up into heaven, where I saw my father Abraham. I bowed before him, and he greeted me with kindness. All the saints honored me because I was his son. They walked with me and brought me to the Lord. I worshiped with them, and the sound of praise filled the air: "You are holy, You are holy, You are holy, Lord of all. Heaven and earth are filled with Your glory."

The Lord spoke to my father from His holy place, saying, "Welcome, Abraham, my faithful servant. It is good that you've come to this holy city. You may ask anything in the name of your beloved son Isaac, and I will give it to you."

Abraham answered, "All power belongs to You, Lord Almighty."

The Lord said, "Anyone named after Isaac should write down his last instructions and honor them. On Isaac's special day, let them give bread to a poor person in his name. I will consider them your children in My kingdom."

Abraham asked, "What if someone can't write down the instructions? Will You still accept them in Your mercy?"

The Lord replied, "If they feed a poor person in Isaac's name, I will give them to you as your children in My kingdom. They will join you in the first hour of the thousand-year reign."

Abraham asked again, "What if someone is too poor to buy bread?"

The Lord answered, "If that person stays awake through Isaac's night of remembrance, I will count them as your child and give them a place in My kingdom."

Abraham then said, "What if someone is too weak to stay awake? Will You still accept them in Your love?"

The Lord said, "If they offer even a small amount of incense in Isaac's name, they will be counted as your child. And if they have no incense, let them find Isaac's last words and read them. If they can't read, let them listen to someone else read them. If they can't do that, let them go into their house and say a hundred prayers. Then I will still count them as your child in My kingdom."

"But the most important thing," the Lord continued, "is that they offer a sacrifice in Isaac's name, because Isaac himself was offered as a sacrifice. And I won't just give you those named after Isaac. I will also give you anyone who does any of these good things—who cares about Isaac's life and his message, who shows kindness by giving even a cup of water, who writes out his message by hand, or who reads it with a heart full of faith, truly believing every word. My power, and the power of My beloved Son, and the Holy Spirit will be with them. I will give them to you as sons in My kingdom. Peace to you all, My saints."

When He finished speaking, songs of praise rang out again: "You are holy, You are holy, You are holy, Lord of all. Heaven and earth are filled with Your glory."

Then the Father said to Michael, "Michael, My servant, go quickly. Gather all the angels and saints so they can welcome My beloved Isaac."

Michael sounded his trumpet. All the saints came together with the angels and went to where Isaac was lying. The Lord rode His heavenly chariot, led by the seraphim and surrounded by angels. When they reached Isaac, the Lord turned His joyful face to him.

Isaac cried out, "It's so good that You've come, my Lord! And You too, great archangel Michael! And my father Abraham, and all the saints!"

Then Jacob leaned down and hugged his father. He kissed him and cried. Isaac looked into his eyes and gently motioned for him to be quiet. Then Isaac turned to the Lord and said, "Please remember my beloved Jacob."

The Lord replied, "My power will always be with him. And when the time comes for Me to become human, die, and rise again on the third day, I will make sure everyone remembers your name, and they will call you their father."

Isaac said to Jacob, "My dear son, this is my final instruction for you: always be careful with your actions. Don't dishonor others, because every person is made in God's image. Whatever you do to others, God will do to you when you meet Him. This is where life begins and ends."

After Isaac spoke these words, the Lord gently took his soul from his body. It was as bright and pure as snow. The Lord welcomed it, placed it in His chariot, and carried it up to heaven. The seraphim played music, and the angels and saints celebrated. The Lord gave Isaac the joys of His kingdom forever and promised to grant all the requests Abraham had made. It became an everlasting promise.

This is how our father Isaac left this world. It happened on the twenty-fourth day of the month Mesore. The day when his father Abraham once offered him as a sacrifice was the eighteenth of Mechir (February 12). At Isaac's passing, heaven and earth were filled with a sweet and comforting scent, like the finest silver. This was the fragrance of Isaac's life, offered up to God.

When Abraham offered him, the sweet smell of his sacrifice rose up into heaven. Blessed is anyone who does something kind in the name of these great ancestors. They will be considered sons in the kingdom of heaven. God made an eternal promise to Abraham and Isaac: anyone who performs an act of mercy on their special days will belong to them in heaven forever. They will join the thousand-year reign promised by our Lord, our Savior Jesus Christ, through whom all glory is given to God the Father and the Holy Spirit, who gives life to everything and is united with the Father and the Son, now and forever. Amen.

Testament of Jacob

In the name of the Father, the Son, and the Holy Spirit—the one true God.

With God's help, we begin telling the story of our ancestor Jacob, son of Isaac. This was written on the twenty-eighth day of the month of Misri. May his prayers protect us from all evil. Amen.

He said, "Come close, my beloved family and friends who love God. Listen to what has been passed down to us."

When Jacob, the faithful son of Isaac and grandson of Abraham, became very old and was close to dying, God sent the angel Michael to him. The angel said, "Jacob, also called Israel, you are deeply loved and chosen by God. The time has come to write down your final words. Give instructions to your family and prepare your home. Soon, you'll join your ancestors and celebrate with them forever."

Jacob, who often spoke with angels, answered, "Let God's will be done."

God blessed Jacob. He had a private place where he prayed every day and night. Angels often came to visit, protect, and strengthen him. When Jacob moved to Egypt to see his son Joseph, God helped him and made his family grow. Although Jacob had cried so much that his eyesight had become poor, it returned when he saw Joseph. He bowed, hugged Joseph, kissed him, and said, "Now I can die peacefully, because I've seen your face again, my beloved son."

Joseph continued to lead Egypt, while Jacob lived in Goshen for seventeen more years. He always followed God's laws and respected Him. But he became very old, and his eyesight faded so badly that he could no longer see anyone clearly.

One day, Jacob looked toward the light of heaven and became afraid. The angel said, "Don't be scared, Jacob. I've been with you since you were born. I'm the one who said you would receive the blessings of your father and mother. I protected you from Laban when he chased you and gave you his wealth. I blessed your family and animals.

"I also saved you from Esau and was with you when you came to Egypt. You became the father of a great nation. Your grandfather Abraham was called God's friend because of his kindness. Your father Isaac pleased God and was offered to Him in faith. And you, Jacob, saw God with your own eyes. You saw the angel, the ladder reaching to heaven, and the Lord sitting above it. You said, 'This is God's house, the gate of heaven.' You are truly blessed. Don't be afraid.

"Your descendants will always be known as the fathers of the faith. Blessed are the people who follow your example. Blessed are those who do kind things in your name—like giving water, helping the poor, welcoming strangers, visiting the sick, or giving clothes to those in need. Whoever writes, reads, or listens to your story with faith will be forgiven and welcomed into God's kingdom.

"Jacob, your time of pain is over. You will now enter eternal peace, a place filled with mercy, light, and joy. Say your final words to your family. Peace be with you. I must return to the One who sent me."

When the angel finished, he rose into heaven. Jacob thanked and praised God. His whole family gathered around him in tears, saying, "You're leaving us! What will we do in this foreign land?"

Jacob comforted them. "Don't be afraid," he said. "God appeared to me in Upper Mesopotamia and told me not to worry. He promised to stay with me and with all of you forever. This land will belong to you and your descendants. Don't fear going to Egypt. There, God will make your family large and strong. Joseph will be with me when I pass. Later, you will return here and live in peace."

Knowing the end was near, Jacob called Joseph and said, "If you truly love me, promise to bury my body in our family tomb." Joseph replied, "I'll do exactly as you say." Jacob asked him to swear, and Joseph did. Jacob was satisfied.

Later, someone told Joseph that Jacob was very sick. Joseph brought his sons, Ephraim and Manasseh, to see him. "These are my sons, born in Egypt," he said. Jacob said, "Bring them close to me." He couldn't see well due to old age.

Joseph brought them forward. Jacob kissed them, then asked them to bow. He placed his right hand on Ephraim and his left on Manasseh, even though Manasseh was the older one. Then he said, "May the God who helped my fathers and protected me all my life bless these boys. May my name and the names of Abraham and Isaac be with them always."

Then Jacob told Joseph, "I'm going to die soon. But all of you will return to the land of our fathers. God will be with you. And you, Joseph, will receive a special blessing. I give you the land I won from the Amorites with my sword and bow."

Jacob called all his sons together to tell them what would happen in the future. They gathered in order, from the oldest to the youngest. He spoke to each one about their future and gave them a final blessing.

After resting for a while, Jacob had a frightening vision. He saw many terrifying beings prepared to punish sinners. These included people who were unfaithful in marriage, those who acted inappropriately, those who practiced magic, worshiped idols, or told harmful lies. Their punishment was a never-ending fire and total darkness, where people would cry and grind their teeth.

Then Jacob was taken up to heaven. Everything there was bright and full of happiness. He saw Abraham, Isaac, and the joyful place waiting for those who are saved. When he returned, he gave instructions for his burial in the land of his ancestors. Then he died at the age of 147.

The Lord came with angels Michael and Gabriel to carry Jacob's soul to heaven. Joseph had his father's body embalmed, which took forty days. After that, the family mourned for eighty more days.

Even Pharaoh cried for Jacob because he cared deeply for Joseph. Joseph spoke to Pharaoh's officials and asked them to tell the king that Jacob had made him promise to bury him in Canaan. Pharaoh agreed and said, "Go in peace and keep your promise." He gave Joseph the best horses and chariots.

Joseph thanked God, then left with his brothers, Pharaoh's officials, and many others. It was a large group, like an army, moving through the land. They crossed the Jordan River and mourned for Jacob for seven days. The local people were amazed and said, "This is a great mourning by the Egyptians."

Jacob was buried in Canaan in the tomb Abraham had bought from Ephron near Mamre. After the burial, everyone returned to Egypt. Joseph continued to lead the nation for many years after Jacob's death, staying in Egypt while his father rested with his ancestors.

This is the story that has been passed down to us—Jacob's final days and how his family mourned him. It was written in the sacred books by our holy ancestors.

If you want to know more about Jacob, read the Old Testament. Moses, the first prophet and lawgiver, wrote about him. There, you'll learn how God and His angels stayed close to Jacob, guiding him and speaking with him often.

God once promised, "I will bless your children like the stars in the sky." Jacob told Joseph, "God appeared to me in Canaan and said, 'I will bless you, make you a great nation, and your descendants will live on forever.'"

These teachings were passed down by our holy fathers. Let's live with the same faith, kindness, and love that they had so we can be called their children in God's kingdom. May they pray for us and help us escape the punishment of hell.

Jacob warned his sons about sin and called them the "sword of the Lord." He taught them to show mercy and love, because mercy can save people and cover many sins. Helping the poor is like lending to God.

So, my dear children, don't stop praying or fasting. Keep living by your faith, and you'll push evil away. Stay away from anger, evil actions, and injustice. People who live in sin will not enter God's kingdom.

Honor the saints, because they will speak for you. Be kind to strangers, just as Abraham and Isaac were. Help the poor, and God will feed you with the bread of life. Clothe those in need, and God will clothe you with glory. Read God's word, and remember the saints and their stories. Their names are written in the book of life, and they will celebrate with the angels in heaven.

Remember our holy fathers every year on the twenty-eighth of Misri. This tradition comes from the writings of our ancestors. Through their prayers, we will receive a place in God's kingdom.

We pray that Jesus the Messiah, our Lord and Savior, will forgive our sins and be kind to us on the day of judgment. May He welcome us joyfully, saying, "Come, blessed ones, take the kingdom prepared for you since the beginning of the world."

May He help us understand His truth, forgive us, and save our souls. May He protect us from evil and let us stand by His side on the final day. Through the prayers of His holy mother and all the saints and martyrs, may we also be saved.

Amen, amen, amen. All praise to God—always and forever.

Testaments of the Twelve Patriarchs
(Reuben through Benjamin, in order)

Introduction

The twelve books in this collection are biographies written between 107 and 137 B.C. They show how a skilled Pharisee used the names of some of history's greatest figures to share important lessons. These figures, known as the Twelve Patriarchs, were highly respected leaders of their time.

Each Patriarch tells his life story in these writings. As they lay on their deathbeds, they gathered their children, grandchildren, and great-grandchildren to share their wisdom. They spoke with complete honesty, hoping to guide their families toward a righteous life. If a Patriarch had made mistakes, he openly admitted them and warned his descendants not to follow the same path. If he had lived a good and faithful life, he explained how his choices brought him blessings.

Beyond their personal stories, these writings provide an incredible glimpse into the early belief in a coming Messiah, more than a century before Christ. Another important aspect of this collection is its moral teachings. As Dr. R.H. Charles noted in his study of ancient Jewish writings, the ethical lessons in these texts had a lasting impact. They shaped not only the thinking and language of the New Testament writers but, at times, even the teachings of Christ Himself. These moral lessons go beyond those in the Old Testament while still remaining true to its message, creating a connection between Old and New Testament values.

The influence of these writings on the New Testament is especially clear in the Sermon on the Mount, which reflects their ideas and even uses some of their phrases. The Apostle Paul also seems to have been deeply influenced by these writings, using their ideas and language so often that it is possible he carried a copy with him on his journeys.

This collection of writings is unique because it combines a simple, direct style with deep spiritual meaning. These texts played a key role in shaping the moral and religious ideas that later influenced the Bible.

Testament of Reuben

The Firstborn Son of Jacob and Leah.

Chapter I.

Reuben, the oldest son of Jacob and Leah, was a man who had learned many lessons in life. He wanted to share his wisdom about avoiding temptation, especially the dangers of giving in to desire. He taught how young people can easily make mistakes and how they can protect themselves from falling into sin.

This is the record of Reuben's final words, including the advice he gave to his children before he died at the age of 125.

Two years after his brother Joseph passed away, Reuben became very sick. When his sons, grandsons, and great-grandsons heard about his illness, they gathered to see him one last time. Knowing his time was short, Reuben called them together and said, "My children, my life is coming to an end, and I will soon go the way of my ancestors."

His brothers Judah, Gad, and Asher also came to visit him. Reuben asked them, "Help me sit up, so I can share something I have kept in my heart for a long time. My time to leave this world is near."

After they helped him up, he kissed them and said, "Listen carefully, my brothers, and you, my children, pay attention to my words."

"I call upon God as my witness today—do not follow the sins of youth. Do not fall into temptation as I once did, when I defiled my father Jacob's bed. Because of my sin, God punished me with a painful illness that lasted seven months. If my father Jacob had not prayed for me, I would not have survived."

"I was thirty years old when I committed this terrible sin before the Lord. For seven months, I was seriously ill, barely clinging to life. Afterward, I repented deeply. For seven years, I fasted and prayed, refusing wine, strong drinks, and anything enjoyable. I did not eat meat or allow myself any pleasure, because my sin was so great—something never seen before in Israel."

Reuben continued, "Now, my children, let me tell you what I learned during my time of repentance about the seven spirits of deception that mislead people."

"There are seven spirits that try to lead people into sin, especially when they are young. But at the same time, seven other spirits were given to humans at creation, which allow them to do good."

1. The first is the spirit of life, which gives strength to the body.

2. The second is the spirit of sight, which brings desire.

3. The third is the spirit of hearing, which allows people to learn.

4. The fourth is the spirit of smell, which enables breathing and the enjoyment of scents.

5. The fifth is the spirit of speech, which allows people to share knowledge.

6. The sixth is the spirit of taste, which makes eating and drinking possible, giving energy.

7. The seventh is the spirit of reproduction, which is meant for love and family but can also lead people into temptation.

"This seventh spirit, though last in creation, is the strongest in youth. It often leads young people into sin without them realizing it, like an animal blindly walking toward a cliff. There is also an eighth spirit, the spirit of sleep, which brings rest but also reminds us of death."

Reuben warned, "These good spirits exist alongside spirits that cause people to sin. The first is the spirit of desire, which takes control of the senses and the body's natural urges. The second is the spirit of greed, which causes people to crave more than they need. The third is the spirit of anger, which is tied to bitterness and jealousy. The fourth is the spirit of deception, which makes false kindness seem real. The fifth is the spirit of arrogance, which leads people to become boastful and proud. The sixth is the spirit of lying, which causes dishonesty, jealousy, and betrayal. The seventh is the spirit of injustice, which leads people to steal and take what does not belong to them. Finally, the spirit of sleep, when mixed with these, confuses young minds and leads them away from truth and God's commandments—just as it happened to me."

"That is why, my children, you must love the truth. It will protect you and keep you safe. Listen to your father, Reuben. Stay away from temptation, do not interfere with another man's wife, and avoid getting caught up in dangerous situations with women."

Reuben then shared his personal experience: "If I had not seen Bilhah bathing in a secluded place, I would never have fallen into such a terrible sin. My mind was overwhelmed by what I saw, and I could not sleep until I acted on my thoughts. When our father Jacob left to visit Isaac in Ephrath near Bethlehem, Bilhah drank too much wine and fell asleep uncovered in her room. I went in, saw her, and committed a great sin without her knowing."

"An angel of God revealed my sin to my father Jacob. He was heartbroken because of me and made a vow never to be with Bilhah again. That is why I warn you, my children—do not let yourselves fall into temptation, because it only leads to regret and destruction."

Chapter II.

Reuben continued sharing his experiences and advice with his children.

"My sons, do not let yourselves be distracted by the beauty of women or become too focused on them. Instead, live with pure hearts, honoring and respecting the Lord. Use your energy to do good, learn, and take care of your work until the Lord chooses a wife for you. That way, you will not face the struggles I did."

"Until my father passed away, I was too ashamed to look him in the eye or speak freely with my brothers. Even now, my conscience still troubles me because of my mistake. But my father was compassionate and prayed for me, asking the Lord to forgive me. The Lord showed me mercy, and His anger was taken away."

"From that time forward, I have been careful and have not sinned again. That is why I urge you, my children, to follow what I have taught you, so you do not fall into the same trap."

"Fornication is a trap for the soul. It pulls people away from God and leads them toward sin. It clouds the mind and weakens good judgment, dragging young men into ruin. It has destroyed many throughout history. No matter if a man is old or young, rich or poor, fornication brings shame and makes him an object of scorn."

"Look at the example of Joseph. He resisted temptation, avoided sinful thoughts, and kept his heart pure. Because of this, he found favor with both God and man. An Egyptian woman tried everything to make him sin. She used magic, false promises, and even trickery, but Joseph stayed strong and did not give in. Because of his faithfulness, God protected him and saved him from hidden danger."

"If you do not allow desire to take over your heart, no evil power can control you. Women, my children, often fall into this sin and use deception to mislead men. Since they do not have the physical strength to overpower men, they rely on their beauty and charm to get what they want. If that does not work, they use more subtle tricks."

"An angel of the Lord revealed to me that women are often more tempted by the spirit of fornication than men. In their hearts, they plan ways to capture a man's attention, using their looks and dress to deceive. First, they take hold of a man's thoughts with their beauty. Then, with a simple glance, they plant temptation in his heart. Once his will is weakened, they trap him in sinful actions. Women cannot force men openly, but they lure them in with their behavior."

"So, my children, avoid fornication at all costs. Teach your wives and daughters not to dress or act in ways that deceive or tempt others. Women who rely on these tricks will face judgment. This same sin led the Watchers astray before the flood. When these heavenly beings saw women and desired them, they changed their forms and pursued them, even though the women were married. The women gave in to temptation and had children with them—giants of great size and strength, almost reaching the heavens."

"Protect yourselves from this sin. If you want to keep your hearts pure, be careful with what you allow yourself to see and hear. Teach women to be modest in how they act around men so they, too, can stay pure in mind and heart. Even if there is no outright sin, too much closeness and familiarity can lead to destruction."

"Fornication does not bring wisdom or godliness. It only causes confusion, jealousy, and rivalry. Because of this, you will become jealous of the sons of Levi and try to elevate yourselves above them, but you will fail. God will defend them, and those who oppose them will face a bitter end."

"God has given leadership to Levi, along with Judah, myself, Dan, and Joseph. But Levi has been given the knowledge of God's law, the authority to judge Israel, and the responsibility to offer sacrifices until the end of time. He will serve as the Lord's High Priest."

"I urge you, by the God of heaven, to be honest with each other and to love your brothers. Respect Levi and approach him with humility so that you may receive his blessing. Levi will bless both Israel and Judah because the Lord has chosen him to be a spiritual leader and king over the nation. Honor his descendants, for they will fight battles for you—both physical and spiritual. And from his family line, an eternal King will come and live among you."

With these words, Reuben finished his teachings. Shortly after, he passed away. His sons placed his body in a coffin and carried it from Egypt to Hebron, where they buried him in the cave beside his father.

Testament of Simeon

The Second Son of Jacob and Leah.

Chapter I.

Simeon, the second son of Jacob and Leah, was known for his great strength. However, he struggled with jealousy and played a major role in the plan against Joseph.

This is what Simeon told his sons as he neared the end of his life at 120 years old, the same year his brother Joseph passed away. When Simeon became seriously ill, his sons gathered around him. Gathering his strength, he sat up, embraced them, and began to speak:

"Listen carefully, my children, to the words of your father, Simeon. I want to share the thoughts that weigh on my heart. I am Jacob's second son, and when I was born, my mother Leah named me Simeon because the Lord heard her prayer. From a young age, I was given great strength. I feared nothing and was never afraid of a challenge. But my heart was hard, my spirit was stubborn, and I lacked compassion."

"God gives people strength, both in body and in spirit, as He chooses. In my youth, jealousy overshadowed my strength. I was filled with envy toward Joseph because our father loved him more than the rest of us. I let this jealousy grow inside me, and I set my heart against Joseph, determined to destroy him. The prince of lies, working through the spirit of jealousy, blinded me. I stopped seeing Joseph as my brother and never considered how much pain I was causing our father, Jacob."

"But the God of Joseph and our ancestors stepped in. He sent His angel to protect Joseph from my hands. I remember the day I went to Shechem to bring ointment for the flocks, and Reuben traveled to Dothan to gather supplies. During that time, Judah sold Joseph to the Ishmaelites. When Reuben found out what happened, he was devastated because he had planned to bring Joseph back to our father."

"When I learned that Judah had let Joseph be taken away alive, I was furious. For five months, I was filled with anger toward Judah for what he had done. But in His mercy, the Lord stopped me from acting on my rage. To humble me, God made my right hand wither for seven days. This suffering helped me realize that I was being punished for what I had done to Joseph."

"I repented with all my heart. I cried, begged for forgiveness, and promised to turn away from envy, impurity, and foolishness. I finally understood that my sin was not just against Joseph but also against the Lord and my father, Jacob."

"So, my children, I beg you to listen carefully to what I am saying. Protect yourselves from envy and deception. Envy can take over a person's heart completely, leaving no room for peace or happiness. It can steal your appetite, make you restless, and drive you to destroy the person you envy. As long as that person succeeds, the envious one remains miserable."

"For two years, I fasted and humbled myself before the Lord in repentance. Only through the fear of God was I freed from envy. When a person trusts in the Lord, the evil spirit of jealousy leaves them, and their heart becomes lighter."

"Once I was freed from envy, I began to feel love and compassion toward Joseph. I forgave him, and I was finally at peace. That is why I urge you to stay away from envy, my children. Only by trusting in God and keeping your hearts free from jealousy can you truly be happy."

Chapter II.

Reuben, the oldest son of Jacob, gave advice to his children and those who would listen, warning them to guard their hearts against jealousy and envy.

"My father once asked me why I always seemed troubled. He saw the sadness in me and wanted to know what was wrong. I told him, 'I am hurting in my liver.' But the truth was, my sorrow ran much deeper than any physical pain. I was carrying the guilt of helping sell my brother Joseph.

When we went to Egypt and Joseph, disguised as an Egyptian ruler, accused me of being a spy and had me tied up, I didn't argue or resist. I knew in my heart that I deserved this. It was a punishment for what I had done.

But Joseph was a man of great kindness, filled with the Spirit of God. He held no grudge against me or any of our brothers. Even after everything we did to him, he still loved us. He treated me like his own family and never sought revenge.

My children, learn from this and protect yourselves from jealousy and envy. Be honest and have a pure heart. Those who live with integrity receive God's grace, honor, and blessings—just like Joseph did. You saw how, despite everything that happened, he never spoke harshly to us. Instead, he loved us deeply, even more than his own children. He gave us wealth, land, and livestock, showing kindness beyond what anyone could expect.

That is why I tell you to love each other sincerely. Let love fill your hearts, and envy will not be able to take hold of you. Envy is like a disease—it eats away at the soul, weakens the body, and stirs up anger. It leads to hatred, violence, and even death. It clouds the mind, fills a person with rage, and causes them to lose control.

Even when a jealous person sleeps, they are not at peace. Like an evil spirit, envy torments the soul, confuses the mind, and disturbs the body. It never stops, always pushing a person toward misery. Wherever envy exists, peace disappears.

Look at Joseph as an example. He was strong, noble, and full of grace because there was no wickedness in him. A person's face often reflects what is inside them, and Joseph's goodness could be seen in his appearance.

Now, my children, keep your hearts pure before the Lord and live honestly with others. If you do this, you will be blessed by God and respected by people. Be especially careful to avoid fornication, for it leads to all kinds of evil. It separates people from God and pulls them toward sin.

I have read in the writings of Enoch that in the future, some of your descendants will fall into fornication and violence, bringing harm to the descendants of Levi. But know this: they will not defeat Levi, for he will rise with the strength of the Lord and fight for what is right. He will overcome all opposition and win the battles that come against him.

In the future, the tribes of Israel will be divided, and only Levi and Judah will remain together. Among your descendants, no one will hold lasting power, just as our father Jacob prophesied. So, my children, take these words to heart. Learn from my mistakes, walk in the ways of righteousness, and do not fall into the traps of envy and sin."

Chapter III.

A prophecy of the coming of the Messiah.

"I have shared all these things with you, my children, so that I am not responsible for any wrongdoing you may commit. If you let go of jealousy and stubbornness, my name will be remembered in Israel like a blooming rose, and my life will be honored in Jacob like a fragrant lily. My memory will be as sweet as the scent of Lebanon, and from my family, strong and holy leaders will rise like mighty cedar trees. Their influence will spread far, and they will endure for generations.

During that time, the descendants of Canaan will disappear, and there will be no survivors among the people of Amalek. The people of Cappadocia will be wiped out, and the Hittites will be completely destroyed. The land of Ham will fall, and its people will vanish.

Then, the earth will finally know peace. The troubles that plague it will come to an end, and wars will cease. The Mighty One of Israel will honor the descendants of Shem, and the Lord God will come to earth to save humankind.

On that day, all lying and deceitful spirits will be crushed and cast away. Wickedness will no longer have power over people, and their suffering will end. When that time comes, I will rejoice and praise the Most High for His great works. I will glorify Him because He will have taken on human form, walked among people, eaten with them, and saved them through His power.

Now, my children, listen carefully. Show respect to the tribes of Levi and Judah, and follow their leadership. Do not rise against them, for from these two will come God's salvation. From Levi, the Lord will bring forth a High Priest, and from Judah, a King—both fully God and fully human. Through them, He will rescue all nations and the people of Israel.

I am giving you these instructions so that you will pass them down to your children and ensure they are followed for generations. Teach them to walk in the ways of the Lord and to honor His plan for salvation.

After Simeon finished speaking, he passed away at the age of 120 years. His sons placed his body in a wooden coffin, planning to carry his remains to Hebron. However, during a war with the Egyptians, they secretly moved his bones because the Egyptians kept a tight guard over Joseph's remains, storing them in the royal tombs.

Egypt's sorcerers had predicted that if Joseph's bones were taken away, a terrible plague would strike their land. Darkness and despair would spread across Egypt, and even with a lamp, people would not be able to recognize their own brothers.

Simeon's sons mourned their father deeply. They remained in Egypt until the time of their great departure, when the Lord kept His promise and, through Moses, led His people to freedom."

Testament of Levi

The Third Son of Jacob and Leah.

Chapter I.

Levi, the third son of Jacob and Leah, was known for his deep spiritual nature, dreams, and prophetic visions. This is the message he gave to his sons, instructing them on how to live and revealing what would happen to them in the future.

Levi was still strong and healthy when he gathered his children because he had been told that his time on earth was coming to an end. When they were all together, he said:

"I, Levi, was born in Haran and later traveled with my father Jacob to Shechem. When I was around twenty years old, I joined my brother Simeon in seeking justice against Hamor and the men of Shechem for dishonoring our sister, Dinah.

Later, while taking care of the flocks in Abel-Maul, the Lord gave me wisdom and understanding. I realized how deeply people had fallen into sin, turning away from what is right. I saw that arrogance had built high walls, and lawlessness ruled from great towers. My heart was troubled, and I prayed to the Lord for help.

As I prayed, I fell into a deep sleep and saw myself standing on a high mountain. Suddenly, the heavens opened, and an angel of God appeared, calling out to me, 'Levi, come forward!'

I followed the angel and was taken up to the first heaven, where I saw a vast sea floating in the air. Amazed, I was then led higher to the second heaven. This place was much brighter, filled with an overwhelming light that stretched endlessly in every direction.

I turned to the angel and asked, 'Why is this heaven so much brighter than the first?' The angel replied, 'Do not be surprised, for you will go even higher and see a place far greater than this. There, you will stand near the Lord. You will serve Him, reveal His mysteries to people, and announce the coming of the One who will save Israel.'

Then the angel said, 'Through you and Judah, the Lord will make Himself known among people, bringing salvation to all nations. The Lord Himself will provide for you—He will be your inheritance, your land, your vineyard, and your wealth.'

The angel then explained what I had seen in the heavens. 'The first heaven looks dark to you because it records all the sins of people. It contains fire, snow, and ice, prepared for the day of God's judgment. There, the spirits of punishment wait for the time when they will carry out God's justice.

The second heaven is where the armies of heaven stand, ready for the day of judgment. They will bring justice against the forces of evil and deception. Above them are the holy ones, set apart by God.

The highest heaven of all is the dwelling place of God's great glory, far above all others in holiness. Just below it is the place where the archangels live. These powerful beings serve before the Lord, praying for the righteous and offering atonement for sins committed in ignorance. Their sacrifices to God are pure and pleasing, requiring no blood.

Below the heaven of the archangels, another group of angels carries messages to those who stand in God's presence. Further down are the thrones and dominions—beings who never stop praising and glorifying God.

When the Lord looks upon creation, everything shakes. The heavens, the earth, and even the deep places tremble before His majesty. Yet people, unaware of these things, continue to sin and offend God without realizing the seriousness of their actions.'"

With these words, Levi finished describing his vision. He urged his sons to live with an awareness of God's power and to take responsibility for the knowledge He had given them.

Chapter II.

Levi spoke with deep passion, urging his sons to stay faithful and seek wisdom, preparing for the day when the Lord will bring judgment.

"My children, understand this—one day, the Lord will judge all people. On that day, the earth will tremble, rocks will split, the sun will grow dark, water will dry up, and even fire will shrink away in fear. Everything in creation will be shaken, and even the hidden spirits will disappear. The underworld will claim those it has taken, and the Most High will bring His power upon the world. Yet, even when these terrifying signs appear, some people will still refuse to believe. They will harden their hearts and continue in their wickedness.

Because of their stubbornness and sins, they will receive the punishment they deserve. But the Most High, in His mercy, has heard your prayers and chosen you to live apart from wickedness. He has called you to be His servant, standing in His presence to do His work.

You are to share wisdom with Jacob's people and shine like the sun for all of Israel's descendants. A great blessing will rest on you and your family, lasting until the day the Lord shows His mercy to all nations and extends His promise forever.

That is why the Lord has given you wisdom and understanding—so that you may teach these truths to your children. Those who honor the Lord will be blessed, but those who reject Him will bring destruction upon themselves.

In a vision, an angel appeared and opened the gates of heaven for me. I saw the holy temple, and on a glorious throne sat the Most High, shining in splendor. He spoke to me, saying, 'Levi, I have given you the blessing of the priesthood. Your descendants will serve Me until the time when I come to live among My people.'

Then, the angel led me back to earth and placed a shield and a sword in my hands. He told me, 'You must bring justice to Shechem for what was done to your sister Dinah. Do not be afraid, for I will be with you. The Lord Himself has sent me to you.'

Following the Lord's command, I led the battle against the sons of Hamor, just as it was written in the heavenly records. Afterward, I asked the angel, 'Tell me your name so I may call on you when I need help.'

The angel answered, 'I am the one who prays for the people of Israel, making sure they are not completely destroyed. Evil spirits are always trying to harm them, but I protect them.'

When I woke up from this vision, I gave thanks and praise to the Most High for His amazing works. I also blessed the angel who prays for Israel and all who follow the Lord, amazed at God's mercy and His care for His people."

Through this powerful story, Levi reminded his children of the importance of their calling and the need to live with faith, righteousness, and obedience to the Lord.

Chapter III.

Levi shared his visions, revealing the incredible rewards that await those who live righteously. His words came from both personal experience and divine revelations.

"When I was returning to my father, I found a bronze shield on a mountain, which I named Aspis. This place is near Gebal, south of Abila. I kept this moment in my heart, thinking about it deeply. Not long after, I advised my father and my brother Reuben to command the sons of Hamor not to be circumcised. My anger burned against them because of what they had done to my sister Dinah.

In my fury, I struck down Shechem first, and Simeon killed Hamor. After that, our brothers joined us, and together we destroyed the city with our swords. When my father Jacob found out, he was deeply troubled. He was upset that the men of Shechem had been circumcised only to be killed afterward. He looked at Simeon and me with disappointment, and we realized that we had disobeyed his will. That day, he became ill with sorrow.

However, I understood that God's judgment had come upon Shechem for their evil ways. They had planned to treat Sarah and Rebecca with the same dishonor they inflicted on Dinah, but the Lord stopped them. Their sins did not start with us—they had troubled Abraham when he stayed in their land, harassing his flocks and mistreating his household. They did the same to all travelers, stealing their wives and dishonoring them. Because of their wickedness, God's punishment fell on them.

I told my father, 'Through you, the Lord will remove the Canaanites from this land and give it to your descendants.' From then on, Shechem became known as the city of fools because they had brought destruction upon themselves.

After we left Shechem, we traveled to Bethel. Seventy days later, I had another vision, similar to the first one I had seen. In my dream, seven men dressed in white robes came to me. They said, 'Levi, rise and put on the robe of the priesthood, the crown of righteousness, the breastplate of understanding, the garment of truth, the plate of faith, the turban for your head, and the ephod of prophecy.'

Each man carried a sacred item, and they placed them on me one by one. Then they declared, 'From now on, you and your descendants will serve as priests to the Lord forever.'

The first man anointed me with holy oil and gave me the staff of judgment. The second man washed me with pure water, gave me bread and wine, and dressed me in a glorious robe. The third man clothed me in a linen vest similar to an ephod. The fourth wrapped a purple sash around my waist. The fifth gave me a branch from a rich olive tree. The sixth placed a crown on my head. Finally, the seventh man placed a priestly diadem on me and filled my hands with incense to offer before the Lord.

Then they spoke, saying, 'Levi, your descendants will be divided into three groups, each carrying a part of the Lord's glory. The first group will be the greatest of all. The second will hold the sacred priesthood. The third will take on a new name because a king will come from Judah and establish a new priesthood, following the ways of the nations. He will be greatly honored because He will be a prophet of the Most High, from the family of Abraham, our ancestor.'

They finished by saying, 'Everything good in Israel will be given to you and your descendants. You will enjoy the Lord's blessings, and your family will serve His people at His holy table.'"

Levi shared his visions and teachings with his children, giving them guidance for their lives and revealing the sacred role their family would play in God's plan.

"Among your descendants, some will become high priests, judges, and scribes. They will be responsible for protecting and keeping the holy place sacred. When I woke up from my dream, I realized it was similar to my first vision. I kept this knowledge in my heart and told no one.

Two days later, Judah and I traveled with our father Jacob to visit our grandfather Isaac. While we were there, Isaac blessed me according to the visions I had seen. He spoke prophetic words over me but chose not to continue the journey with us to Bethel.

When we arrived in Bethel, my father Jacob had a vision about me. In it, he saw that I was meant to serve as a priest for our people. The next morning, he got up early and gave his tithes to the Lord through me, marking the beginning of my sacred calling. From there, we traveled to Hebron and settled there.

Isaac often called me to his side and reminded me of the law of the Lord, as it had been revealed to him and our ancestors. He taught me about the priestly laws and the different kinds of sacrifices—burnt offerings, firstfruits, freewill offerings, and peace offerings. Every day, he instructed me on these sacred duties and prayed for me before the Lord.

Isaac also warned me, saying, 'Be careful of the temptation of impurity, for it will continue through your descendants and bring sin into the holy place.' He advised me to marry a woman of good character, someone pure and without corruption, and not to marry anyone from the foreign nations. He stressed the importance of remaining clean, telling me to wash before entering the holy place, to cleanse myself before making sacrifices, and to wash again after completing the sacrifices.

He also instructed me, 'Take branches from twelve trees that have leaves and offer them to the Lord, as Abraham taught me. From every clean animal and bird, bring sacrifices to God. Offer the firstfruits of your harvest and wine as offerings. And remember, every sacrifice must be seasoned with salt.'

I told my children to follow these commands, saying, 'Everything I have learned from my ancestors, I now pass on to you. I will not be responsible for the sins you commit in the future, especially those against the Savior of the world, Christ. You will act without respect, deceive Israel, and bring great troubles upon it from the Lord. Because of your disobedience, the Lord will no longer protect Jerusalem. The veil in the temple will be torn apart, and your shame will be exposed to the world.'

I warned them further, 'You will be taken as captives among the nations, suffering disgrace because of your actions. However, the city the Lord has chosen will still be called Jerusalem, as it is written in the book of Enoch, the righteous one.'

I shared details of my own life, saying, 'When I was twenty-eight years old, I married a woman named Melcha. She gave birth to my first son, whom I named Gersam, because we were strangers in a foreign land. I had a vision that Gersam would not rise to the highest position among my descendants.

When I was thirty-five, my second son, Kohath, was born at sunrise. In a vision, I saw him standing in an important role among our people, so I named him Kohath, meaning "the beginning of greatness and wisdom."

At forty, my wife gave birth to my third son, Merari, but his birth was very difficult, and she almost died. Because of this, I named him Merari, which means "my sorrow." When I was sixty-four years old, in Egypt, my youngest daughter, Jochebed, was born at a time when I was highly respected among my brothers.

Gersam had two sons, Lomni and Semei. Kohath's sons were Amram, Issachar, Hebron, and Ozeel. Merari's sons were Mooli and Mouses. When I was ninety-four, my grandson Amram married my daughter Jochebed; they were born on the same day.'

I reflected on my life's journey, saying, 'I was eight years old when I entered the land of Canaan, eighteen when I fought against Shechem, and nineteen when I became a priest. At twenty-eight, I got married, and at forty-eight, I moved to Egypt. Now, my children, you are the third generation after me, and in my one hundred and eighteenth year, your uncle Joseph passed away.'

Levi's words were filled with history, visions, and important lessons. He gave his descendants a guide for their future, urging them to stay faithful to God's covenant and to live righteously.

Chapter IV.

Levi spoke with deep wisdom and concern, urging his children to live righteously and wisely while warning them about the consequences of turning away from God. His words were meant to guide them toward a life that honors the Lord and avoids the dangers of sin and rebellion.

"My children, I urge you to fear the Lord with all your heart and follow His law completely. Let your respect for God guide every decision you make, and treasure His commandments above all else.

Teach your children to read and write, so they can understand and carry God's law with them throughout their lives. A person who knows and follows God's law will be respected wherever they go. They will never feel like a stranger, for wisdom brings honor and recognition.

A wise and righteous person will gain more friends than even their parents could provide. Many will seek to serve them, listen to their words, and learn about God's teachings from them. Living righteously is like storing up treasure in heaven, where it is safe forever. If you fill your hearts with goodness, you will enjoy its rewards. But if you fill them with evil, you will only bring trouble upon yourselves.

Seek wisdom with all your heart and trust in God. Unlike wealth, land, or power, wisdom cannot be stolen by enemies or lost in exile. The only things that can destroy wisdom are the blindness that comes from wickedness and the hardness of heart caused by sin. If you protect yourself from these, wisdom will always be your strength, even in difficult times. In a foreign land, wisdom will feel like home, and even among enemies, it will be your ally.

Those who teach truth and live by it will be honored like kings, just as my brother Joseph was. Because of his wisdom and righteousness, Joseph was given great authority and respect.

But my children, I see that in the future, you will turn away from the Lord. You will choose wickedness, and because of your sins, people will mock and despise you. Even though our father Israel remains faithful and pure, the leaders of our people will dishonor our family by mistreating the Savior of the world.

Just as the heavens are purer than the earth in God's eyes, you are meant to be a light to Israel, shining brighter than the nations around you. But if you allow sin to darken your hearts, what hope will there be for those who are already lost in spiritual blindness? By rejecting God's law and creating your own rules, you will bring a curse upon our people.

You will steal what belongs to the Lord, taking offerings meant for Him and wasting them on sinful pleasures. Out of greed, you will twist God's commandments to suit your desires. You will dishonor married women, take advantage of young women, and form sinful relationships. You will marry foreign women and perform false rituals to justify your actions, repeating the sins of Sodom and Gomorrah.

Because of your pride in your priesthood, you will think you are above others, even above God's commands. You will mock what is holy, treating sacred things with laughter and disrespect. Because of this, the Lord will destroy the temple He has chosen, and you will be taken as captives to foreign lands.

Other nations will despise you and mock you. You will bear the shame of God's punishment, and those who hate you will celebrate your downfall. If it weren't for the mercy promised to Abraham, Isaac, and Jacob, not a single one of our descendants would remain on the earth.

For seventy weeks, you will turn away from righteousness, corrupting the priesthood and defiling the sacrifices. You will ignore God's law and reject His prophets. You will mistreat the righteous and hate those who follow God, despising the words of truth.

Then, when a man comes to restore God's law with the power of the Most High, you will call him a liar. You will refuse to recognize who He truly is and will plot to kill Him, staining your hands with innocent blood. Because of this, your holy places will be destroyed, left in ruins.

You will have no place of safety, and you will be scattered among the nations, living under a curse. But one day, the Lord will show mercy again. He will welcome those who turn back to Him in faith, washing them clean and restoring them to His covenant."

Levi's words were both a warning and a promise. He urged his descendants to choose wisdom and righteousness, but he also spoke of God's mercy, which would one day bring them back to Him.

Chapter V.

As you have heard about the seventy weeks, now listen to what will happen with the priesthood. In every generation, there will be priests. In the first generation, the first priest will be great and will speak to God as a son speaks to his father. His priesthood will be perfect before the Lord, and on the day of his greatest joy, he will rise up to bring salvation to the world.

In the second generation, the chosen priest will come from a time of sorrow among loved ones, and his priesthood will be honored and praised by many. The third priest will suffer greatly. The fourth will also endure pain, as wickedness will rise against him, and all of Israel will be filled with hatred, with people turning against each other.

The fifth priest will live in a time of darkness, and the same will happen in the sixth and seventh generations. By the seventh generation, corruption will be so terrible that words cannot even describe it, but those who commit such evil will understand the full weight of their actions. Because of their sins, they will be taken captive, and their land and possessions will be destroyed.

In the fifth week, they will return to their ruined land and rebuild the house of the Lord. By the seventh week, priests will appear who are corrupt, greedy, and immoral. They will worship idols, commit adultery, steal money, act arrogantly, break the law, and defile even children and animals. Because of their evil, the Lord will punish them, and the priesthood will come to an end.

Then, the Lord will raise up a new priest. To this priest, all of God's words will be revealed. He will bring justice to the earth for many days. His star will shine in the heavens like a king's star. He will spread knowledge of the Lord like sunlight covering the earth, and he will be praised throughout the world.

He will shine like the sun, removing all darkness from under the sky. Peace will cover the earth. The heavens will rejoice in his days, and the earth will be glad. Even the clouds will celebrate. The knowledge of the Lord will spread across the earth as abundantly as the waters of the sea.

The angels in heaven will rejoice because of him. The heavens will open, and holiness will come upon him from the temple of glory. The voice of the Father will declare his name, just as it was spoken to Abraham and Isaac. The Most High will reveal his glory over him, and the spirit of wisdom and holiness will rest upon him through water.

He will share the greatness of the Lord with His people forever. No one will take his place for all generations. Through his priesthood, knowledge will spread among the nations, and they will come to know the grace of the Lord. Under his priesthood, sin will come to an end, and lawlessness will be destroyed.

He will open the gates of paradise, removing the sword that blocked the way since the time of Adam. He will allow the righteous to eat from the tree of life, and the spirit of holiness will rest upon them. He will defeat the power of Beliar and give his followers the strength to overcome evil.

The Lord will take joy in His people and be pleased with His chosen ones forever. Abraham, Isaac, and Jacob will rejoice, and I too will be glad, as all the saints are filled with joy.

Now, my children, you have heard everything. It is your choice whether to walk in the light or stay in darkness, whether to follow the law of the Lord or the ways of Beliar.

His sons responded, "We will walk before the Lord and follow His law." Their father said, "The Lord is our witness, His angels are witnesses, and you are witnesses, as I am, to the promise you have made today."

His sons answered, "We are witnesses."

Then Levi finished speaking to his sons. He lay down on his bed, stretched out his feet, and passed away at the age of one hundred and thirty-seven. They placed him in a coffin and later buried him in Hebron with Abraham, Isaac, and Jacob.

The Testament of Judah

The Fourth Son of Jacob and Leah.

Chapter I.

Judah, the fourth son of Jacob and Leah, spoke to his sons before he passed away, sharing his experiences and the lessons he had learned.

"My children, listen to the words of your father, Judah. I was the fourth son born to my father Jacob, and my mother Leah named me Judah, saying, 'I give thanks to the Lord for blessing me with another son.'

In my youth, I was strong, fast, and always obedient to my father. I showed great respect to my mother and her sister. When I became a man, my father blessed me, saying, 'You will be a king and will succeed in everything you do.' The Lord favored me in all my work, both in the fields and at home.

Once, I chased a deer, caught it, and prepared it as a meal for my father, who was pleased. I became skilled in hunting and could outrun and capture any animal in the plains. I even caught and tamed a wild horse.

I once killed a lion and saved a young goat from its jaws. I grabbed a bear by its paw, threw it over a cliff, and crushed it. I outran a wild boar and tore it apart while running. A leopard once attacked my dog in Hebron, but I grabbed it by the tail, slammed it against the rocks, and killed it.

I also came across a wild ox feeding in the fields. I grabbed it by the horns, swung it around, and struck it down. When two kings of the Canaanites came armed to attack our flocks, I faced them alone. I struck the king of Hazor on his armor, pulled him down, and killed him. The king of Tappuah, who was on horseback, I also struck down, scattering his army.

I fought Achor, a giant warrior who threw spears from horseback. I lifted a heavy stone, threw it at his horse, and killed it. I battled him for two hours, broke his shield, cut off his feet, and defeated him. As I was removing his armor, nine of his men attacked me. Wrapping my garment around my arm, I fought back with stones and killed four of them. The rest fled.

My father Jacob once killed Beelesath, the king of all the kings, who was twelve cubits tall and incredibly strong. Fear spread among our enemies, and they stopped waging war against us. My father had no fear in battle when I was with him because he had seen a vision of a powerful angel protecting me, ensuring I would never be defeated.

A greater war than the one at Shechem came upon us in the south. I joined my brothers in battle, chasing a thousand men and killing two hundred, including four kings. I climbed the city wall and killed four strong warriors. We captured Hazor and took its treasures.

The next day, we marched to Aretan, a heavily fortified city that was a threat to us. Gad and I attacked from the east, while Reuben and Levi came from the west. The men on the wall, thinking we were alone, came down to fight us. Meanwhile, my brothers secretly climbed the wall, entered the city, and struck down the warriors.

We burned their tower and took control of the city. As we were leaving, the men of Tappuah attacked, trying to steal our spoils. We fought them, defeated them, and reclaimed everything. At the waters of Kozeba, the men of Jobel waged war against us. We defeated them and their allies from Shiloh, making them too weak to attack us again.

On the fifth day, the men of Makir came to take our spoils. We met them in battle, overcame their strongest warriors, and killed them before they could retreat up the hill. When we reached their city, the women rolled stones down from the hilltop to stop us. Simeon and I circled behind the town, took the high ground, and destroyed the city.

The next day, we learned that the king of Gaash was advancing with a powerful army. Dan and I disguised ourselves as Amorites and entered their city as allies. In the middle of the night, our brothers arrived, and we opened the gates for them. We defeated the men, destroyed their defenses, and took their possessions.

We then moved to Thamna, where the treasures of many enemy kings were stored. When they insulted us, I became angry and charged up the hill, even as they threw stones and arrows at me. Dan came to help, and together we drove them away. They fled and later fought my father Jacob, but he made peace with them. We did not harm them further, and they became subject to us. We returned their possessions and restored order.

I built Thamna, and my father built Pabael. I was twenty years old during these wars, and the Canaanites feared me and my brothers. I had many herds and put Iram the Adullamite in charge of them. While visiting him, I met Parsaba, the king of Adullam. He welcomed us and hosted a great feast.

During the feast, he gave me his daughter Bathshua as my wife. She bore me three sons: Er, Onan, and Shelah. However, the Lord took the lives of Er and Onan, leaving only Shelah, whose descendants remain with you now."

Chapter II.

For eighteen years, my father Jacob lived in peace with his brother Esau and Esau's sons after we returned from Mesopotamia, where we had stayed with Laban. But when those eighteen years passed, in the fortieth year of my life, Esau and his men attacked us with a strong and well-armed army.

During the battle, my father Jacob shot an arrow at Esau, wounding him. Esau was taken back to Mount Seir, where he later died at a place called Anoniram. We chased after Esau's sons, who had built a city with iron walls and brass gates. Since we couldn't break through, we set up camp around the city and laid siege to it.

For twenty days, they refused to open the gates. Then, in full view of everyone, I climbed a ladder with my shield protecting me, while they threw large stones down at me. Even though the stones were heavy, I managed to kill four of their strongest warriors. Reuben and Gad killed six more. After this, the people inside the city surrendered and asked for peace. After speaking with our father, we agreed to make them our subjects. They were required to send us five hundred cors of wheat, five hundred baths of oil, and five hundred measures of wine every year. This continued until the famine forced us to go down to Egypt.

Later, my son Er married Tamar, a woman from Mesopotamia and a daughter of Aram. But Er was a wicked man and treated her badly because she was not from Canaan. Three days after their wedding, an angel of the Lord struck him down. He had never been with her because his mother had convinced him not to let Tamar bear his children.

During the wedding, I gave Tamar to my other son, Onan. But Onan also acted wickedly. He lived with her for a year but refused to be with her properly. When I confronted him, he pretended to listen, but he still disobeyed. He wasted his seed instead of allowing her to conceive, following his mother's instructions. Because of this, the Lord struck him down too.

I planned to give Tamar to my youngest son, Shelah, as his wife, but his mother refused. She schemed against Tamar because she disliked her for not being a Canaanite, just as she herself was. I knew the people of Canaan were wicked, but in my youth, I had been blinded by my desires.

She tricked me into marrying her by getting me drunk on wine, even though my father Jacob had not approved. While I was away, she secretly arranged for Shelah to marry a Canaanite woman. When I found out, I was heartbroken and angry. In my grief, I cursed her. Her wickedness eventually led to her death, as well as the deaths of her sons.

Meanwhile, Tamar remained a widow. After two years, she heard that I was going to shear my sheep, so she dressed herself as a bride and sat at the city gate in Enaim. Among the Amorites, it was a custom for a woman about to marry to sit at the gate for seven days.

I was drunk with wine and did not recognize her. Her beauty deceived me, and I approached her, saying, "Let me be with you." She asked what I would give in return, and I handed her my staff, my belt, and my royal diadem as a pledge. I was with her that night, and she became pregnant.

Later, not knowing what had happened, I wanted to punish her and even considered putting her to death. But she secretly sent back my pledges, proving that I was the one responsible. This shamed me deeply. When I summoned her, she repeated the private words I had spoken to her when I was drunk. I realized this was from the Lord and could not harm her.

I thought she might have acted cleverly, but she had taken the pledge directly from me, not from someone else. From that moment on, I never went near her again, knowing I had committed a terrible mistake.

The people of the city claimed that no prostitute had been at the gate because Tamar was not from the city and had only stayed there briefly. I thought my actions had gone unnoticed.

After this, we went down to Egypt because of the famine. I was forty-six years old when we arrived there, and I lived in Egypt for seventy-three more years.

Chapter III.

Listen carefully, my children, and follow my advice. Obey God's laws and keep His commands. Do not let your desires or pride lead your decisions. Do not brag about your strength or accomplishments, because such arrogance is not pleasing to God.

I used to think I was strong enough to resist temptation. I even scolded my brother Reuben for his sin. But jealousy and desire tested me, and I made mistakes with Bathshua, a Canaanite woman, and Tamar, who was meant to marry my sons.

When I wanted to marry Bathshua, I told her father I would first ask my own father. But he didn't want to wait. Instead, he showed off his wealth and offered it in her name. He was a king, and he covered her in gold and jewels. Then, at a feast, he gave us wine and used her beauty to tempt me.

The wine clouded my judgment, and my desires took over. I fell in love with her, slept with her, and broke God's commands. I married her, but God punished me for my mistakes. I found no happiness in the children she gave me.

So, my children, I warn you: do not drink too much wine. It confuses the mind and stirs up dangerous desires. It makes you see things the wrong way and weakens your self-control. Wine can trick you into thinking you are happy while it actually leads you to sin.

When a man gets drunk, his mind fills with sinful thoughts, and his body craves wicked things. If the opportunity arises, he will sin without shame. A drunk person loses all respect for others.

I let wine lead me into sin. I publicly shamed myself and my family when I turned to Tamar. I ignored God's laws and married a Canaanite woman, which was against His will.

Be very careful with wine. Drink only in moderation, with respect for God. If you go too far, it will control your mind and fill you with deceit. A drunk man speaks shameful words, sins without regret, and even thinks his disgrace is something to be proud of.

A man who gives in to desire is blind to what he is losing. Even a king who falls into lust will lose his power and become a slave to his own urges. I know this from experience. When I gave Tamar my staff, my belt, and my crown, I lost symbols of my strength and honor.

I repented, but I suffered greatly. From that time on, I avoided wine and meat for the rest of my life, and I found little joy. God's angel showed me that women can have power over all men—kings, warriors, and even the poor. They can take away a king's glory, a strong man's power, and a poor man's last bit of hope.

So, my children, remember the dangers of wine. It carries four great evils: lust, reckless desire, foolishness, and greed. Drink with joy, but always with respect for God. If you forget Him while drinking, you will fall into sin.

If you truly want to live righteously, it is better to avoid wine completely. Drunkenness leads to fights, insults, and rebellion against God. It can ruin your life too soon. Wine also makes people reveal secrets—both human and divine. I foolishly told God's commandments and my father Jacob's wisdom to Bathshua, though I was not supposed to.

Wine causes confusion and conflict. My children, I warn you: do not let greed or attraction control you. These things led me astray, and

I know they will bring trouble to my descendants. Because of them, Judah's kingdom will suffer, even though God blessed me with it for obeying my father.

I never disobeyed my father Jacob. I followed all his commands, and my grandfather Isaac blessed me to be king over Israel. Jacob confirmed this blessing. I know my family's kingdom will continue, but I also know the sins you will commit in the future.

Beware of lust and greed. These sins will turn you away from God, blind your soul, make you arrogant, and destroy your kindness. They fill your life with stress and misery, robbing you of peace. They stop you from worshiping, make you forget God's blessings, and turn you against His teachings.

A man controlled by these desires cannot serve God. He walks in darkness, even in daylight. Greed is like idolatry—it makes people trust money instead of God and drives them to madness.

Because of money, I lost my children. If I had not repented and prayed, I would have died without a family. But God showed me mercy because I sinned in ignorance. I was blinded by deception, and through my mistakes, I learned how weak I truly was.

My children, understand that two spirits guide every person: the spirit of truth and the spirit of deceit. In between is the spirit of understanding, which helps a man choose his path. Everything we do is recorded in our hearts, and God sees it all.

No deed is hidden from Him. The spirit of truth witnesses everything, and a sinner is judged by his own heart, unable to lift his face before God.

The Testament of Issachar

The Fifth Son of Jacob and Leah.

Chapter I.

Issachar, the fifth son of Jacob and Leah, was known for his humble nature and simple way of life.

He gathered his sons and said, "Listen to me, your father Issachar, and pay attention to my words, for I am loved by the Lord. I was born as Jacob's fifth son because my mother made a deal with Rachel in exchange for mandrakes.

One day, my brother Reuben found mandrakes in the field. Rachel saw them and took them, which upset Reuben, and he cried loudly. My mother, Leah, heard his cries and came outside. Mandrakes are fragrant fruits, similar to apples, that grow near water in the land of Haran.

Rachel refused to give them back, saying, 'I need these as a substitute for the children I have not had. God has not given me any sons.'

There were two mandrakes, and Leah argued, 'Isn't it enough that you took my husband? Now you want these too?' Rachel replied, 'I will let you have Jacob with you tonight in exchange for the mandrakes.'

Leah insisted, 'Jacob is my husband. I was with him from the beginning.' But Rachel said, 'Don't be so proud. Jacob worked fourteen years to marry me, and I was meant to be his wife before you. If it weren't for the lies and deceit of others, you would not have been given to him instead of me. My father tricked both of us that night. If I had been there, none of this would have happened.'

Despite this, Rachel said, 'For the sake of the mandrakes, I will give Jacob to you for one night.' That night, Jacob was with Leah, and she became pregnant with me. Since she had used the mandrakes to secure time with Jacob, she named me Issachar.

Later, an angel appeared to Jacob and told him, 'Rachel will have two sons because she has chosen to live in self-control rather than chasing after Jacob with selfish desires.' If Leah had not given up the mandrakes to be with Jacob, she would have had eight sons instead of six. The Lord allowed Rachel to have two children because of the mandrakes.

God saw that Leah wanted to be with Jacob not for her own pleasure but to continue his family line. Because of her selflessness, I was born, and Jacob's family continued to grow."

The next day, Rachel once again allowed Leah to be with Jacob because of the mandrakes. Though she had wanted them, Rachel did not eat them. Instead, she offered them to God and gave them to the priest at the Lord's house.

As I grew up, my children, I lived an honest and simple life. I worked in the fields for my father and brothers, harvesting food at the right times. My father saw my integrity and blessed me.

I never meddled in others' affairs or felt jealous of my neighbors. I did not gossip or judge how others lived. I kept my heart pure and my conscience clear.

When I turned thirty-five, I got married. By then, years of work had worn me down, and I had not spent my time chasing pleasure or thinking about women. I was so focused on my work that I would often fall asleep exhausted.

My father, Jacob, was proud of me because I always gave the first portion of my harvest to God through the priest and then brought the rest to him. The Lord blessed my efforts, and my crops multiplied greatly. My father knew this was because my heart was pure and honest before God.

I shared freely with the poor and those in need, always giving with kindness and sincerity.

Now, my children, listen to me and live with honesty and integrity, for I have seen how much the Lord loves those with pure hearts. Such people do not crave riches or take advantage of others. They are not obsessed with fine food or luxury. They do not fear death but trust in God's plan for their lives.

Those with pure hearts cannot be controlled by deceitful spirits. They avoid looking at things that could lead them into temptation or corrupt their thoughts. They do not hold grudges, feel jealous, or become consumed by worldly desires.

They live truthfully, guided by a clear conscience. They avoid sin and stay faithful to God's commandments.

So, my children, obey God's laws and live with honesty and simplicity. Do not interfere in other people's business. Instead, love God and care for those around you. Show kindness to the poor and weak.

Work hard, especially in farming, and always give thanks to God for your blessings. Offer the first part of your harvest to Him, and He will reward you, just as He has blessed His faithful servants since the time of Abel.

Remember, the land itself is your inheritance. It will provide for you through hard work.

Jacob, our father, blessed me with the abundance of the earth, and God showed His favor by giving me good harvests. Among our family, the Lord gave special roles to Levi and Judah. Levi was chosen to serve as a priest and lead our people spiritually. Judah was given the role of ruler and protector of Israel.

Honor and respect these chosen ones of the Lord. Live with the same sincerity and integrity that I have shown, for it is through a pure heart that God's blessings will remain with you.

Know that Gad has been chosen by God to protect Israel. He will rise up against our enemies and keep our people safe, as the Lord has commanded.

Chapter II.

Your descendants will one day turn away from the simple and pure way of life that pleases the Lord. Instead of being content, they will always want more, chasing after their desires without satisfaction.

They will abandon honesty and sincerity, choosing instead to follow deceit and evil. Ignoring God's commandments, they will be drawn toward wickedness, following the path of the deceiver. Hard work and caring for the land will no longer matter to them. Instead, they will focus only on their own selfish plans.

Because of these sins, they will be scattered among foreign nations and forced to serve their enemies. Their disobedience will take them far from God's blessings, and they will suffer under those who rule over them.

So, my children, teach these warnings to your own children. If they fall into sin, they must return to the Lord quickly. God is merciful and full of compassion. If they cry out to Him, He will hear them, free them from their suffering, and bring them back to their land—if they truly repent.

I am now 126 years old, and I stand before you with a clear conscience. As far as I know, I have not committed any sin. I have been faithful to my wife and have never been with another woman. I never let my eyes lead me into lust or sin.

I avoided drinking wine, so it would not cloud my judgment. I did not desire what belonged to others, and I never allowed deceit to take root in my heart. I have never spoken lies.

Whenever I saw someone struggling, I shared in their pain and sorrow. I gave food to the poor and lived with kindness and faith in

God every day. I have always walked in truth, loving the Lord with all my heart and treating others with the same sincerity and care.

My children, I urge you to live as I have. If you follow this way of life, every evil spirit will flee from you, and no wicked person will have power over you. Even wild animals will not harm you, because the God of heaven and earth will be with you. You will live among others with honesty and a pure heart.

After saying these things, I gave my last instructions to my sons. I told them to carry my body to Hebron and bury me in the cave with my ancestors. Then, having spoken my final words, I lay down peacefully and passed away. I lived a long life, still strong in body, and entered the eternal rest that the Lord had prepared for me.

The Testament of Zebulun

The Sixth Son of Jacob and Leah.

Chapter I.

Zebulun, the sixth son of Jacob and Leah, shared his final teachings with his sons two years after Joseph's death, at the age of 114.

He gathered his children and said, "Listen to me, my sons, and hear the words of your father, Zebulun. When I was born, I was a blessing to my parents. After my birth, my father Jacob's wealth increased greatly. His flocks and herds multiplied, especially because of the striped rods he used to claim his share of the livestock.

Throughout my life, I have not knowingly committed any sins, except for those in my thoughts. Even then, I can only recall one major wrongdoing—the time I went along with my brothers in keeping Joseph's fate a secret from our father. In my heart, I grieved for many days, but I was too afraid to speak up. My brothers had made a pact that anyone who revealed the truth would be killed.

When they first plotted to kill Joseph, I begged them with tears not to do such a terrible thing. Simeon and Gad were ready to strike him down, but Joseph pleaded with them, saying, 'Please, my brothers, have mercy on me! Think of our father Jacob and do not spill innocent blood. I have done nothing against you. If I have sinned, then punish me, but do not take my life—it would break our father's heart.'

His cries were unbearable. I wept with him, my heart aching so much that I could barely stand. Joseph saw me crying beside him, and when he realized that our brothers were closing in to kill him, he ran behind me for protection, begging me to save him.

At that moment, Reuben stepped in and said, 'Do not kill him. Instead, throw him into this dry pit.' These pits had been dug by our forefathers but had never filled with water. By God's design, this saved Joseph's life.

My brothers agreed and threw Joseph into the pit. Later, they sold him to the Ishmaelites. I took no part in the money they received for him, but Simeon, Gad, and six of our other brothers used it to buy sandals for themselves and their families. They said, 'We will not eat food purchased with this money, for it was paid with our brother's blood. Instead, we will walk on it, just as Joseph claimed he would rule over us. Let's see what happens to his dreams now.'

Their actions were later reflected in the law of Moses, which says that if a man refuses to raise children for his brother, his sandal should be taken from him, and he should be publicly shamed. In the same way, our brothers rejected Joseph, and God stripped them of the authority they had once held over him.

Years later, when they arrived in Egypt, Joseph's servants removed their sandals at the palace gates, and they bowed before him as they would before Pharaoh. Not only did they bow, but they were also humiliated, spit upon, and forced to the ground in shame. When the

Egyptians learned how they had treated Joseph, they condemned them for their cruelty.

After selling Joseph, my brothers sat down to eat and drink, but I could not bring myself to join them. I felt too much pity for Joseph. Instead, I stayed near the pit, afraid that Simeon, Dan, or Gad might try to harm him. Seeing that I would not eat, my brothers put me in charge of watching over him until the Ishmaelites arrived.

When Reuben returned later and found out that Joseph had been sold, he tore his clothes in grief and cried, 'How can I face our father now?' He took the money and ran after the merchants, hoping to buy Joseph back, but he could not find them. They had already taken a shortcut through the land of the Troglodytes. Reuben returned to us heartbroken and refused to eat for the rest of the day.

Dan tried to calm him, saying, 'Do not weep. We have a plan to explain everything to our father. We will kill a young goat and dip Joseph's coat in its blood. Then we will send it to Jacob with the message: Is this your son's coat?'

When Joseph was sold, my brothers took his coat and dressed him as a slave. Simeon kept the coat for himself, refusing to let it go. In anger, he wanted to tear it apart with his sword because Joseph was still alive.

The rest of us turned against Simeon and warned him, 'If you do not hand over the coat, we will tell our father that you alone were responsible for what happened to Joseph.'

Reluctantly, he gave it up, and we carried out Dan's plan. We sent the bloodied coat to Jacob, making him believe that Joseph had been killed by a wild animal."

Chapter II.

Zebulun, the sixth son of Jacob and Leah, urged his children to live with kindness, unity, and mercy, sharing the lessons he had learned throughout his life.

He told them, "My children, I ask you to follow God's commandments. Be kind to your neighbors and show compassion to all living things—not just people, but also animals under your care. Because of this kindness, God has blessed me greatly. When my brothers fell sick, I was the only one who remained healthy, for the Lord sees what is in each person's heart.

Let compassion guide your actions. Whatever kindness you show to others, God will return to you. Many of my brothers' children became ill and died because they lacked mercy for Joseph. But my own children remained healthy, as you yourselves have seen.

When I lived by the sea in Canaan, I became a fisherman to provide for my father Jacob. Many people drowned in the sea, but the Lord kept me safe. I was the first among us to build a boat and sail the waters, for God gave me the wisdom to do so. I designed a rudder to steer the boat and raised a sail on a mast. With these, I traveled along the shores, catching fish to feed our family until we moved to Egypt.

Because of the kindness in my heart, I shared what I caught with anyone in need. If someone was a stranger, sick, or old, I would cook the fish, prepare them well, and offer them to him. I grieved with those who were suffering and tried to ease their burdens. Because of this, God always blessed my fishing. Whoever gives generously to others will receive even more from the Lord in return.

For five years, I fished and gave to the poor, providing enough to sustain not only them but also my father's household. In the summer, I worked as a fisherman, and in the winter, I took care of the sheep alongside my brothers.

There is one act of kindness I want to tell you about. One winter, I saw a man shivering from the cold because he had no clothes. Feeling deep compassion, I secretly took a garment from my father's house and gave it to him. My children, let this be an example for you. From everything God gives you, be quick to show kindness. Give freely to anyone in need with a willing and joyful heart.

Even if you have nothing to give, do not turn away from those who are suffering. Walk with them, share in their pain, and let them know they are not alone. There was a time when I had no way to help a man in distress, so I walked beside him for seven furlongs, crying with him and wishing I could ease his burden.

My children, be compassionate to everyone, and God will be compassionate to you when you are in need. In the last days, He will pour out His mercy upon the earth, and wherever He finds hearts filled with kindness, He will be with them. God's mercy for a person will always match the mercy they have shown to others.

Remember Joseph. Even after all we did to him, he did not seek revenge. Follow his example. Be free of hatred, love one another, and do not hold grudges. Resentment destroys families, troubles the soul, and weakens the spirit.

Think about how a river flows. When its waters are united, they are strong enough to carry stones, trees, and even the earth itself. But when the river breaks into small streams, the water dries up and disappears. The same will happen to you if you let divisions grow among you.

Do not let yourselves be torn apart. Everything in creation has one head and works together as a single body—two shoulders, two hands, two feet, and so on. I have read in the writings of my ancestors that Israel will one day be divided. You will follow two kings and commit terrible sins. Because of this, your enemies will take you captive, and you will suffer among foreign nations, facing disease and hardship.

But even then, you will remember the Lord and repent. He is merciful and forgiving. He does not hold onto anger forever, knowing that people are weak and easily led astray. When you return to Him, the Lord will rise as the light of righteousness. You will return to your land and see Him in Jerusalem, for His name's sake.

Yet even after this, you will fall into sin again and make Him angry. He will cast you away until the time comes for everything to be fulfilled.

Now, my children, do not be sad that my time is near. Do not grieve because I am leaving you. I will rise again among my descendants as a ruler, and I will rejoice with those in my tribe who follow God's commandments. But for those who choose wickedness, the Lord will bring eternal fire, and their families will be destroyed.

My time has come to rest, just as it did for my fathers before me. Honor the Lord with all your strength and remain faithful to Him throughout your lives."

After saying these words, Zebulun passed away peacefully at an old age. His sons placed his body in a wooden coffin and later carried him to Hebron, where they buried him with his ancestors.

The Testament of Dan

The Seventh Son of Jacob and Bilhah.

Chapter I.

Dan, the seventh son of Jacob and Bilhah, spoke these words to his sons near the end of his life when he was 125 years old.

He gathered his family and said, "Listen closely, my sons, to the words of your father. Pay attention to the lessons I share, for they come from my life's experiences and the truths I have learned. I have seen that honesty and fairness bring blessings from the Lord, while lies and anger lead only to destruction and wickedness.

I must confess to you, my children, that I once allowed jealousy and anger to take hold of my heart. I wanted to kill my brother Joseph, even though he was good and truthful. When he was sold into slavery, I felt joy because I envied him. Our father loved him more than the rest of us, and it hurt my pride. A voice inside me whispered, 'Are you not also Jacob's son? Don't you deserve the same love?'

One of the spirits of deception urged me to take a sword and end Joseph's life. It convinced me that if he were gone, our father would love me more. This was the spirit of anger, pushing me to destroy Joseph, just as a wild animal crushes its prey.

But God did not allow me to carry out my evil plan. I was never able to find Joseph alone, and I was stopped from harming him. If I had succeeded, I would have destroyed one of the tribes of Israel.

Now, as my life comes to an end, I warn you: if you do not guard yourselves against lying and anger, you will destroy yourselves. Anger blinds the heart and mind, making it impossible to see the truth in others.

An angry person treats even his own parents as enemies. He no longer recognizes his own brother, ignores the words of wise men, and has no respect for the righteous. Even a close friend becomes like a stranger to him. Anger traps a person in lies, twisting his thoughts and filling his heart with hatred and jealousy.

My children, anger is a dangerous thing. It takes over the soul and controls the body, pushing it toward wrongdoing. As the body follows anger's commands, the soul becomes blind and starts justifying its actions, believing them to be right.

A man with power who is full of anger is even more dangerous. His rage is strengthened in three ways: first, by those who serve him and carry out his orders; second, by his wealth, which he uses to harm others; and third, by his physical strength, which he uses to do evil.

Even a weak man becomes more dangerous when fueled by anger, because rage multiplies his ability to do harm.

Anger is closely connected to lies, and together they lead people into cruelty and deception. My children, understand that anger is a useless and destructive force. It starts with harsh words, grows into harmful actions, and fills the mind with rage and confusion.

When someone insults you, do not let anger take hold of you. And when someone praises you, do not let it make you proud. Do not let either praise or insult control your emotions, for both can be traps. At first, compliments feel good, making a person search for reasons to feel important. But later, when insulted, an angry person believes his rage is justified.

If you experience loss or hardship, do not let it trouble your heart. Anger uses disappointment to make people crave things they do not have, leading to frustration and rage. Whether you lose something by choice or by accident, do not let it disturb your peace. Frustration fuels anger, and anger invites lies, forming a destructive cycle.

When anger and lies work together, they fill the heart with constant turmoil. A soul caught in this cycle drives away the presence of the Lord, allowing deception to take control instead.

My children, guard your hearts against the power of anger. Instead, choose patience, truth, and kindness, for these are the ways of the Lord. They bring peace and strength to the soul. Anger blinds, divides, and destroys, but righteousness and love bring unity and lasting strength."

Chapter II.

Listen carefully, my children, and take these words to heart. Follow God's commandments and live according to His law. Stay away from anger and the rejection of truth. If you do this, you will create a place where the Lord can dwell among you, and the deceiver, Beliar, will have no power over you.

Always speak truthfully to one another. Truth protects you from confusion and anger. When you live in honesty, you will remain at peace because the God of peace will be with you, and no enemy will be able to defeat you.

Love the Lord with all your heart and soul, and love each other sincerely. This love will unite you and protect you during difficult times.

But I see that in the future, many of you will turn away from God. Some of you will rebel against Levi and fight against Judah, but you will not succeed. An angel of the Lord will guide Levi and Judah, and through their strength, Israel will stand firm.

When you abandon God, you will fall into sin. You will follow the ways of foreign nations, chasing after wickedness and acting without restraint. Pride and deception will lead you into wrongdoing.

I have read in the writings of Enoch, the righteous man, that Satan will work alongside these spirits of evil to corrupt the sons of Levi, leading them to sin against the Lord. My own descendants will also fall into sin and join Levi in their wrongdoings. Meanwhile, the sons of Judah will become greedy, taking what does not belong to them, like lions devouring their prey.

Because of these sins, you will be taken into captivity. You will suffer plagues like those in Egypt and endure hardships under foreign nations. But even in your suffering, if you turn back to the Lord, He will show you mercy. He will bring you home to His sanctuary and restore peace to you once again.

From the tribes of Judah and Levi, the Lord will send a Savior. He will fight against Beliar and defeat him, bringing justice against our enemies. He will rescue the souls of the faithful from the grasp of evil and turn the hearts of the disobedient back to God. Those who call upon Him will find eternal peace.

The righteous will find rest in Eden, and the faithful will rejoice in the New Jerusalem. This city will forever bring glory to God. No longer will Jerusalem be empty, and no longer will Israel be taken captive. The Lord Himself will live among His people. The Holy One of Israel will reign with humility, and those who believe in Him will rule in truth.

Fear the Lord, my children, and be careful not to fall into Satan's traps. Stay close to God and to the angel who watches over you, for he stands between God and man, working for Israel's peace and fighting against the enemy's kingdom.

The enemy wants to destroy those who call on the Lord because he knows that when Israel repents, his power will be broken. The angel of peace will strengthen Israel, preventing them from completely falling into evil, even in times of great corruption.

Even when Israel turns away from righteousness, the Lord will not abandon them forever. Instead, He will reshape them into a nation that fulfills His purpose. His name will be known not only in Israel but also among the nations.

So, my children, stay away from all evil. Let go of anger and lies, and hold onto truth and patience. Live according to the teachings I have given you and pass them down to your children. Then, when the Savior of the nations comes, He will accept you. He is truthful, patient, humble, and kind, teaching the law of God through His actions.

Turn away from wickedness and follow the righteousness of the Lord. If you do this, your descendants will be saved forever.

Bury me with my fathers, for I wish to rest beside them.

After saying these words, he kissed his sons, lay down, and passed away peacefully at an old age. His sons buried him, and later, they carried his bones to be placed near Abraham, Isaac, and Jacob.

Yet, even in his final moments, Dan warned that his descendants would turn away from God. They would lose their place in the land of their ancestors, become distant from the people of Israel, and be cut off from their family's inheritance.

The Testament of Naphtali

The Eighth Son of Jacob and Bilhah.

Chapter I.

Naphtali, the eighth son of Jacob and Bilhah, shared his final teachings with his sons as his life neared its end. At the age of 130, he gathered his children on the first day of the seventh month to pass down his wisdom.

While still in good health, he prepared a feast of food and wine for his family. The next morning, he woke and said, "My time is near." His sons did not believe him because he still appeared strong. But as he praised and glorified the Lord, his strength increased, and he repeated that he would soon pass away. Then, he began to speak:

"My sons, listen to the words of your father, Naphtali. I was born to Bilhah, and Rachel gave me my name. She had given Bilhah to Jacob in her place, and when I was born on Rachel's knees, she named me Naphtali. She loved me dearly and would often kiss me, saying, 'May I one day have a son of my own who is like you.'

Joseph, my brother, was indeed like me, fulfilling Rachel's prayers. My mother, Bilhah, was the daughter of Rotheus, the brother of Deborah, who was Rebecca's nurse. She was born on the same day as Rachel and came from a noble, God-fearing family that descended from Abraham. Rotheus, however, was captured and sold as a slave to Laban. Laban gave him Euna, a servant, as a wife.

Euna gave birth to Zilpah, naming her after the place where Rotheus was captured. Later, she had Bilhah, saying, 'My daughter is quick to take to new things,' because Bilhah eagerly reached for her mother's breast.

Like my mother, I too was swift. I was as fast as a deer, and my father Jacob trusted me to deliver all his important messages. He blessed me as a fast runner, comparing me to a deer.

The Lord is like a potter, shaping each person with care and intention. Every body is designed to match the spirit it holds, and nothing is created without purpose. Everything in creation is made with precision—perfectly measured and balanced.

Just as a potter knows the use of each vessel he makes, God knows the strengths and weaknesses of every person. He sees how far someone will go in righteousness and when they may turn to evil. Nothing is hidden from Him, for He created everyone in His image.

A person's strength reflects their actions. Their eyes affect their rest, and their soul determines the words they speak—whether they follow God's law or the ways of wickedness. Just as light and darkness are separate, so is every person unique, created exactly as God intended.

God made everything in an orderly way. He placed the senses in the head, covering it with hair as a sign of dignity. The neck connects the head to the body, the heart is for wisdom, the stomach for nourishment, the liver for anger, the gall for bitterness, and the spleen for laughter. Every part of the body has a purpose, designed by God's will.

Therefore, my children, let all your actions be done with order and purpose. Do nothing with bad intentions or at the wrong time. Just as an eye cannot hear, you cannot walk in the ways of light while living in darkness.

Guard yourselves against greed and deceitful words that can lead the soul astray. Keep your hearts pure, and know when to remain silent. If you do, you will understand God's will and reject the ways of evil.

The sun, moon, and stars never leave their assigned paths, and neither should you stray from God's commandments. Do not live in disorder, as the Gentiles have done. They have turned away from the

Lord, worshiping idols and following deceitful spirits. Do not be like them. See God's presence in the heavens, the earth, and the seas, and in all creation. Do not follow the ways of Sodom, which went against the natural order.

Even the Watchers, the fallen ones, defied the order God had set for them. Because of their sins, they were cursed and brought destruction to the earth before the flood. I share this warning because I have read in the writings of Enoch that you, too, will one day turn away from God. You will follow the wickedness of the nations and fall into the same sins as Sodom.

Because of this, the Lord will allow your enemies to take you captive. You will suffer, serving foreign nations, until He has humbled you. But when you are reduced in number and remember the Lord, you will return to Him, and in His mercy, He will restore you to the land of your ancestors.

Yet even after returning, you will again forget the Lord and fall into sin. Because of this, He will scatter you across the earth until, in His compassion, He sends a man who will bring righteousness and mercy to both those who are near and those who are far away."

The Testament of Gad

The Ninth Son of Jacob and Zilpah.

Chapter I.

Gad, the ninth son of Jacob and Zilpah, shared his final words with his children as his life neared its end. At the age of 125, he gathered them together to pass down the lessons he had learned, speaking with honesty and a sincere desire to help them avoid the mistakes he had made.

"My sons," he said, "listen to me carefully. I was the ninth son of Jacob, and I was known for my strength and courage as a shepherd. It was my responsibility to guard our flocks, keeping them safe from wild animals. Whenever a lion, wolf, or any predator came near, I would chase it down without fear. I would grab its foot, throw it to the ground, and kill it to protect the flock.

When my brother Joseph came to help tend the sheep, he stayed with us for over a month. But he was young and not used to the heat, so he became sick and returned to Hebron, where our father cared for him with great love. While he was there, Joseph told our father that the sons of Zilpah and Bilhah, including me, were taking the best of the flock and eating them, despite the warnings of Reuben and Judah.

One day, Joseph saw me pull a lamb from the jaws of a bear. Though I killed the bear, I was heartbroken that the lamb did not survive, so we ate it. Joseph reported this to our father, and from that moment, I held resentment toward him. My anger grew stronger over time, and by the day he was sold into slavery, it had completely taken over my heart.

Hatred took root in me, and I no longer wanted to hear Joseph's name or see his face. I hated when he corrected us, and I resented how our father always believed him. The bitterness inside me became so strong that I even wished for his death. My heart was filled with rage, and I wanted him gone, as an ox eats up the grass.

But Judah secretly sold Joseph to the Ishmaelites, and God prevented us from committing an even greater sin. Because of this, Joseph was saved from our hands, and we were spared from committing a terrible crime.

Now, my children, listen to me and choose truth and righteousness. Stay far away from hatred, for it destroys everything good. A person ruled by hatred cannot see clearly and despises even those who do what is right. Hatred poisons the soul, blinds the heart, and fills life with bitterness.

Hatred leads to sin and even rebellion against God. It ignores His command to love others and causes people to act against His will. A person who hates enjoys pointing out the faults of others and takes pleasure in their downfall. Whether toward a friend, a brother, or a servant, hatred brings destruction.

Hatred and envy go hand in hand. A hateful person cannot stand to see others succeed and becomes sick with jealousy at the sight of their prosperity. Love, on the other hand, brings healing, even to those who have sinned. But hatred only seeks to destroy and refuses to show mercy, even for the smallest mistakes.

Hatred works alongside Satan, using anger and reckless actions to bring harm. In contrast, the spirit of love follows God's law, leading to patience and salvation. Hatred creates lies and deception, turning small problems into major conflicts. It twists what is good into something evil and fills the heart with rage, violence, and greed. It corrupts everything it touches and leads only to destruction.

I tell you these things from my own experience, so you will reject hatred and hold on to love. Righteousness drives out hatred, and humility destroys jealousy. A just and humble person is ashamed to act unfairly, for he knows God sees his heart.

A person who fears the Lord will not speak against those who are holy. The fear of God removes hatred, for a righteous person does not want to offend the Lord—not even in his thoughts. These are the lessons I learned after repenting for my hatred toward Joseph.

True repentance removes ignorance and reveals the truth. It opens the eyes, fills the soul with wisdom, and leads the mind toward salvation. Through repentance, a person gains understanding, even without instruction, for God speaks to a humble heart.

The Lord punished me for my sins. I suffered from a disease of the liver, and if not for the prayers of my father Jacob, I would have died. A person is punished in the same way he sins. Because I had harbored cruel anger toward Joseph, I endured severe pain in my liver for eleven months—the same amount of time I allowed hatred to rule my heart.

My children, learn from my mistakes. Choose love, righteousness, and humility instead of hatred and envy. Live according to God's commandments, for they will bring you life and peace."

Chapter II.

Gad, the ninth son of Jacob, spoke to his children with wisdom and a sincere heart, urging them to let go of hatred and embrace love. He had learned from experience how destructive hatred could be, and with deep concern, he shared his final words.

"My children, I beg you to love one another as brothers. Remove all hatred from your hearts. Let your love be shown not only in your words and actions but also in your thoughts and feelings. True love must come from within and spread outward, shaping the way you live.

I must confess that, in front of my father, I spoke kindly to Joseph. But as soon as I was away from him, hatred clouded my mind, filling me with thoughts of harming Joseph. Hatred is a poison that sneaks in unnoticed and takes control, turning even good intentions into evil.

Love each other sincerely, my children. If someone wrongs you, go to them in peace and speak to them with kindness. Do not hold grudges or hide bitterness in your heart. If they admit their fault and ask for forgiveness, forgive them without hesitation. Let love and mercy be stronger than anger and resentment.

If they refuse to admit their wrongdoing, do not let anger take over. Avoid arguing or speaking to them in frustration, as this may cause even more hatred. Your anger might lead them to swear or act out in defiance, and in doing so, you will both fall into sin. Keep your heart calm and trust in God's justice instead of taking matters into your own hands.

Be careful not to share your private thoughts or disputes with others, especially in legal matters. If someone overhears and misunderstands your words, they may turn against you. This could create unnecessary conflict and cause them to sin against you. Many people pretend to offer advice or support, but their true motives may be selfish or deceitful.

Even if someone refuses to acknowledge their wrongdoing, but deep down they feel shame when confronted, do not keep pressing them harshly. They may still find the humility to change and avoid repeating their mistakes. If they truly repent, they may even come to respect you, fear God, and seek peace with you.

But if they remain stubborn and continue in their wrongdoing, forgive them anyway. Let your forgiveness come from your heart, freeing yourself from the burden of anger. Do not seek revenge, for judgment belongs to the Lord alone. Trust that He sees everything and will judge fairly.

My children, hatred only brings pain, separation, and destruction. Love, on the other hand, brings healing, unity, and peace. Forgiveness is not just for the one who is forgiven—it also frees the one who forgives. Trust in the Lord's justice, and let love and mercy guide your actions, even when others do wrong.

If you see another man succeed, do not let your heart be troubled or filled with envy. Instead, pray for him with sincerity, asking the Lord to bless him even more. This will not only bring peace to your soul but also help you grow in righteousness.

If he rises to even greater success, do not let jealousy take hold of you. Remember that life on earth is temporary, and in the end, every person faces the same fate. Instead of being envious, be grateful to God, who gives blessings as He sees fit and provides for all according to His wisdom.

Seek to understand God's ways, and you will find peace of mind and rest for your soul. Trust in His justice and His timing, knowing that His ways are greater than ours.

If someone gains wealth through dishonesty, do not envy them, even if their success seems unfair. Look at the example of Esau, my father's brother—he gathered great wealth, but he did not follow righteousness. Be patient and wait for the Lord's judgment, for He sees everything and will act at the right time.

God, in His mercy, may take away wealth that was gained through sin. If the sinner repents, God will forgive him. But if he refuses to change, his punishment will be eternal, and he will lose not only his wealth but also his soul.

A poor man who lives without jealousy, is content with what he has, and pleases the Lord in all things is more blessed than any rich man. He is free from the worries and temptations that trouble those who chase after wealth without seeking righteousness.

So, my children, remove envy from your hearts and replace it with love. Be honest and sincere in all that you do. Jealousy and envy destroy the soul, but love brings peace, unity, and favor with God.

Teach these lessons to your children so they may also walk in the ways of the Lord. Instruct them to respect Judah and Levi, for through their descendants, the Lord will bring salvation to Israel. These two tribes have been chosen by God for His purpose, and their role in His plan is sacred and everlasting.

Yet, I see that in the future, your descendants will turn away from the Lord. They will fall into sin and bring trouble upon themselves. But even then, God's mercy and justice will remain.

I have spoken to you from my heart. Now, I remind you once more—follow your father's teachings, and when my time comes, bury me with our ancestors. Stay true to the traditions and the God of our fathers in everything you do."

When he finished speaking, he lay down peacefully and passed away. Five years later, his sons carried him to Hebron and buried him with his ancestors, just as he had wished.

The Testament of Asher

The Tenth Son of Jacob and Zilpah.

Chapter I.

Asher, the tenth son of Jacob and Zilpah, gathered his children as he neared the end of his life. At 125 years old, while still strong and healthy, he spoke to them with wisdom, sharing the lessons he had learned.

"My sons, listen carefully to your father, for I want to teach you what is right in the eyes of the Lord. God has given people two choices in life—two paths they can follow, two desires within them, two ways of acting, and two possible outcomes. Everything in life has an opposite, and each person must choose which path to take.

There is the way of good and the way of evil. Within every person, there are two forces—one leading toward righteousness and the other toward sin. If a person chooses to follow goodness, their actions will reflect it. Even if they make mistakes, their heart will lead them to repentance, allowing them to correct their ways and turn back to what is right.

But if someone follows the path of evil, their actions will show it. They will reject what is good, embrace sin, and fall under the influence of wickedness. Even when they try to do something good, their corrupted heart twists their actions toward selfishness and harm.

Some people may appear to be doing good, but if their intentions are selfish or dishonest, their actions will ultimately lead to harm. For example, a person may use others for their own benefit, showing no kindness to those who help them commit wrongdoing. Though they may pretend to do good, their actions are still rooted in evil.

Another example is someone who steals, cheats, or takes from others but then gives to the poor as if they are generous. While charity is good, their kindness is spoiled by dishonesty, making their actions sinful before God.

There are also those who live in sin—committing adultery or other immoral acts—while outwardly appearing religious by fasting or following traditions. Though they may seem devoted, their sinful behavior makes their outward acts meaningless.

People like this are like hares—they may look clean on the outside, but they are unclean in reality. God does not accept such double-mindedness. He calls us to be sincere and whole in our righteousness, not living with divided hearts.

So, my children, do not be like those who try to live in both good and evil. Instead, cling only to what is good, for God dwells in those who are sincere and pure in heart. Wickedness, however, pushes God away and invites evil into a person's life. Those who try to live in both worlds are not truly serving God—they are only serving themselves.

People who are committed to goodness may sometimes be misunderstood or falsely accused by those who are double-minded. But in God's eyes, their actions are righteous. Even if it seems like their choices are complicated, their intentions are pure, and they align with God's will.

Some people choose to completely separate themselves from those who do evil, keeping their bodies and souls undefiled. Though their ways may seem extreme, they show true devotion to God.

Everything in life has an opposite. Within wealth, there is greed. In joy, sorrow can hide. Even in marriage, there can be selfish desires. Life leads to death, honor can turn to disgrace, day gives way to night, and light is followed by darkness. Just as these things are connected, so too does eternal life follow death for those who walk in righteousness.

Truth cannot be changed into a lie, and what is right cannot become wrong. Everything is revealed under the light of God. I have lived my life with this understanding, striving to follow the commandments of the Lord with sincerity. I sought out the truth in all things and did my best to live by it.

My children, take these lessons to heart. Follow God's commandments with complete devotion. Those who are double-minded fall into sin twice over—first, by doing wrong themselves, and second, by encouraging others to sin with them. They align themselves with deceitful spirits and work against righteousness.

Remain steadfast in God's law, rejecting evil and holding on to what is good. When your life comes to an end, you will stand before the angels of God and the forces of darkness. Those who lived in wickedness will be tormented by the evil they served, but those who lived in peace will be led by the angel of the Lord into eternal life.

Do not, my children, be like the people of Sodom, who sinned against God's messengers and were destroyed forever. I know that in the future, you will fall into sin and be taken captive by your enemies. Your land will be ruined, your holy places destroyed, and you will be scattered across the earth like water poured out.

But do not lose hope. The Most High will one day visit the earth. He will come as a man, living among people, eating and drinking with them. He will defeat the power of evil and bring salvation to both Israel and the Gentiles. Through Him, God Himself will speak and act as a man.

Pass these teachings on to your children so they will not turn away from the Lord. I know that many of your descendants will fall into corruption, following human traditions instead of God's law. They will be scattered like Gad and Dan, losing their land, their identity, and even their language. But in His mercy, the Lord will gather them back together through faith, for the sake of Abraham, Isaac, and Jacob.

After saying these things, Asher instructed his sons to bury him in Hebron. Then, he lay down peacefully, passed away, and was buried by his sons alongside his ancestors, just as he had requested.

The Testament of Joseph

The Eleventh Son of Jacob and Rachel.

Chapter I.

Joseph, the eleventh son of Jacob and Rachel, was known for his wisdom, perseverance, and unshakable faith in God. Despite facing betrayal, hardship, and temptation, he remained true to his values. As his life neared its end, he gathered his sons and brothers to share his story and offer them guidance.

"My brothers and my dear children, listen carefully to my words. I, Joseph, was deeply loved by Israel, yet my life was filled with challenges. Let me tell you about my journey, one that tested my faith but was upheld by the truth of the Lord.

Throughout my life, I faced jealousy and even threats against my life. But I never turned away from righteousness. My brothers despised me, but the Lord loved me. They plotted to kill me, yet the God of my fathers protected me. They threw me into a pit, but the Most High lifted me out. I was sold as a slave, yet the Lord set me free.

Though I was taken captive, God's mighty hand rescued me. When I suffered from hunger, He provided for me. When I was alone, He comforted me. In sickness, He healed me. When I was imprisoned, He showed me favor and broke my chains. Though I was falsely accused, He defended me. When the Egyptians spoke against me, the Lord delivered me. Even when other servants envied me, God lifted me up.

Pharaoh's chief officer trusted me and placed me in charge of his household. Everything he owned was under my care. But while I was responsible for all his affairs, I faced my greatest test—the relentless temptation of his wife, who tried to lead me into sin. Yet the God of Israel, the God of my fathers, saved me from falling into that trap.

Even though I resisted her, she had me thrown into prison. I was beaten and humiliated. But the Lord, in His mercy, made me find favor with the prison keeper. No matter how dark my situation seemed, He never abandoned me. Those who fear the Lord are never truly alone—not in trouble, not in chains, not in suffering, and not even in their worst moments.

God is not like humans—He does not grow weak or afraid. He never changes, and His strength supports all who trust in Him. Sometimes, He steps back for a while to test the heart and strengthen the soul. He tested me ten times, and in each trial, I remained faithful. For patience brings great rewards, and endurance leads to countless blessings.

Many times, the Egyptian woman threatened my life. She had me punished, only to later call me back and try again. When I refused her, she tried to persuade me with promises, saying, 'If you give in to me, you will rule over my household. You will have everything my husband owns.'

But I remembered my father's teachings. I ran to my room, wept, and prayed to the Lord. For seven years, I fasted and sought His help. Even though I lived in luxury in the eyes of the Egyptians, inside, I was crying out to God. Those who fast for the Lord are given strength and radiance as a blessing.

When my master was away, I avoided drinking wine. Often, I went three days without eating, giving my food to the poor and sick instead. Every morning, I woke early to pray and grieve over the woman's sinful ways. She would even visit me at night, pretending to care for me.

At first, she acted like a mother, saying she had no children and saw me as a son. I believed her at first and allowed her kindness. But soon, her true intentions became clear—she wanted to lead me into sin.

When I realized her deceit, my heart ached for her, and I prayed for many days.

I tried to teach her about the Most High, hoping she would change her ways. But instead of listening, she flattered me, calling me righteous and holy. In front of her husband, she praised my good character, but in private, she tried to trap me with her words.

Through all of this, the Lord gave me strength. Remember, my children, always put your trust in God. He is faithful and will protect those who honor Him, even in the hardest of trials.

She even tried to convince me by saying, 'Do not be afraid of my husband—he trusts you completely. Even if someone accused you, he would never believe it.' She used these words to tempt me, but they only brought me more pain.

I fell to the ground, crying out to God, begging Him to save me from her deception and keep me from sinning. No matter how many times she tried, she could not break me.

Frustrated, she changed her approach. She came to me again, pretending she wanted to learn about God. She claimed she was ready to leave behind her idols and even said she would convince her husband to do the same if I agreed to be with her.

She disguised her temptation as something righteous, but I saw through her lies. I answered, 'The Lord calls His people to remain pure. He does not accept those who commit adultery. Only those who come before Him with clean hearts and truthful words are pleasing in His sight.'"

Even after everything I said, she remained silent, still scheming to get what she wanted. I dedicated myself even more to fasting and prayer, asking the Lord to protect me from her advances. Then one day, she came to me again and said, "If you refuse to be with me, I will poison my husband and make you my spouse."

Horrified, I tore my clothes and said, "Have fear of God! Do not do something so wicked! You will only bring destruction upon yourself. I will tell everyone about your evil plan." Terrified that I would expose her, she begged me to stay silent.

To win me over, she started sending me gifts and offering me luxuries, trying to tempt me into changing my mind. Then, in desperation, she even tried to use magic against me, mixing enchantments into my food in an attempt to bewitch me.

When her servant brought the food to me, I looked up and saw a vision—an angel handing me a sword along with the meal. I immediately realized that she was trying to deceive me again. As soon as the servant left, I wept bitterly and refused to eat the food she had sent.

The next day, she came to me and asked, "Why haven't you eaten the food I sent?"

I answered, "Because it was poisoned with evil. You told me you wanted to turn away from idolatry and serve the Lord, but your actions show the opposite. The God of my fathers has revealed your wickedness to me through His angel. I kept this knowledge to myself, hoping you would repent."

To show her the power of God, I said, "The evil plans of the wicked cannot harm those who truly serve the Lord. Watch, and I will eat this food before you to prove it." Before taking a bite, I prayed, "O God of my fathers and angel of Abraham, be with me now." Then, I ate.

Seeing this, she fell to the ground, weeping at my feet. I lifted her up and warned her once again to turn away from her sin. She promised she wouldn't do anything evil again, but I could tell her heart was still filled with wickedness. She immediately began looking for another way to trap me.

Her frustration grew, and she pretended to be sick, sighing and moaning to get attention.

When her husband noticed her troubled expression, he asked, "What is wrong? Why do you look so sad?"

She answered, "I feel pain in my heart, and my spirit is heavy." Believing her, he comforted her, not realizing she was lying.

Then, when her husband was away, she came to me again, in a desperate state, and said, "If you do not lie with me, I will take my own life! I will hang myself or throw myself off a cliff."

I saw that she had completely lost control, and that the spirit of Beliar had taken over her thoughts. Distressed, I prayed to the Lord for guidance and strength. Then I turned to her and said, "Why are you in such torment? Why do you let sin blind you? Have you not thought about your children, your future, or what will happen because of your actions? If you take your life, Asteho, your husband's concubine, will mistreat your children and erase your memory from the earth."

Hearing this, she said, "So you do care for me! That alone gives me comfort. If you are willing to look after me and my children, I can accept that for now and hope that one day, my desires will be fulfilled."

But I knew she was still thinking wickedly, twisting my words to fit her own desires.

I did not speak to her out of love but out of obedience to the Lord. When someone is controlled by sinful passion, even the smallest act of kindness is misunderstood and used to fuel their wickedness. Even though I tried to reason with her, she left around midday, still set on getting what she wanted.

I fell to my knees and prayed to the Lord without stopping, crying out to Him all day and night, asking for deliverance from her constant pursuit.

At sunrise, I was still praying and pleading for help.

Then, in her desperation, she made one final attempt. She grabbed my robe and tried to force me to be with her. She held onto my clothes tightly, refusing to let go. Seeing that she would not stop, I pulled away, leaving my robe in her hands. I fled, naked and ashamed, but determined to stay pure.

Enraged and humiliated, she clutched my robe and accused me of attacking her.

When her husband returned, he believed her lies. In his anger, he had me locked in his household prison. The next day, he had me beaten and then sent to Pharaoh's prison.

Even in my suffering, I gave thanks to the Lord. I sang His praises, even in the darkness of my cell. I was filled with joy because God had saved me from falling into sin.

The woman, however, was filled with guilt and sadness. She would visit me in prison and send messages, saying, "If you give in to me now, I will have you released from these chains."

But I never even considered her offer, not even in my thoughts, because I knew it was against the Lord's will.

God values those who remain pure, even in difficult circumstances, more than those who live in luxury but sin. He rewards those who stay faithful and resist temptation. If someone stays righteous and seeks glory for the right reasons, the Most High will honor them in His time.

Many times, even when she was unwell, she would come to my prison, pretending to listen to my prayers. She sighed and moaned, hoping I would change my mind, but I stayed silent.

When I was still in her house, she made bold attempts to tempt me. She dressed in fine clothes, revealing her arms, legs, and chest, using her beauty to try to seduce me. But the Lord, in His mercy, protected me from her tricks. He guarded my heart and body, keeping me from falling into sin.

Chapter II.

Joseph faced many challenges because of a cunning and deceitful woman in Egypt. If you want to see an interesting prophecy, read verses 73 and 74.

My dear children, patience, prayer, and fasting have incredible power. They can change both your heart and your situation. I urge you to stay pure and disciplined, praying and fasting with a humble spirit. When you do this, God will be with you, because He loves those who are pure in heart.

No matter what struggles you face—whether it's jealousy, hardship, or false accusations—God will protect and lift up those who remain pure. He did this for me, and He will do the same for anyone who walks in His ways.

My brothers knew that our father loved me dearly, but I never became proud. Even as a child, I feared God and understood that worldly things do not last forever. I never tried to take revenge on my brothers. When they sold me as a slave, I didn't tell the Ishmaelites that I was the son of Jacob, a powerful man, because I wanted to protect my brothers' honor.

Let this be a lesson to you, my children: always fear God in everything you do, and respect your brothers no matter what happens. Whoever follows God's ways and keeps His commandments will be loved by Him.

When the Ishmaelites took me to a foreign land, they asked if I was a slave. To avoid disgracing my brothers, I told them that I was. One of their elders doubted my words, saying I didn't look like a slave, but I stuck to my story.

When we reached Egypt, they argued about who would buy me. In the end, they agreed to leave me with a merchant until they returned. God gave me favor with this merchant, and he trusted me with his entire household. Because of me, God blessed him, increasing his wealth and prosperity. I stayed with him for a little over three months, and during that time, God continued to bless everything around me.

One day, the wife of Pentephris, a powerful official of Pharaoh, heard about me. She was curious and told her husband about me, saying that I had brought prosperity to the merchant. She suggested that Pentephris take me into his household, believing that my presence would bring them blessings as well.

Pentephris listened to his wife and accused the merchant of kidnapping me from Canaan. The merchant, terrified, fell at his feet and pleaded for mercy, saying he had only been taking care of me until the Ishmaelites returned. Still, Pentephris had him beaten.

Then, Pentephris called for me. I showed him respect because of his high position. He asked if I was a slave or a free man. I told him the truth—I was a slave purchased by the Ishmaelites in Canaan. But he didn't believe me and had me beaten as well.

While I was being punished, the official's wife watched from a window and sent a message to her husband, saying that his judgment was unfair. She argued that I was clearly a free man and had been wrongly enslaved. But Pentephris decided to keep me in prison until the Ishmaelites returned to confirm my story. His wife, however, had another reason for wanting me free—she desired me for herself, though I didn't fully understand her intentions at the time.

After twenty-four days, the Ishmaelites came back. They had learned about my father's sorrow and asked why I had claimed to be a slave when I was really the son of a great man in Canaan. Their words deeply hurt me. I wanted to cry, but I held back my tears so I wouldn't bring shame upon my brothers. Even though I was suffering, I trusted in God's plan.

The Ishmaelites decided to sell me to avoid getting in trouble with my father, Jacob. They feared his power, knowing he was both strong and favored by God. Meanwhile, the merchant, afraid of being punished, asked the Ishmaelites to clear him of guilt. They asked me to say that they had bought me with money so they wouldn't be blamed.

At the same time, the wife of Pentephris urged her husband to buy me. She even sent her servant to purchase me from the Ishmaelites. However, they demanded a high price. Determined, she sent another servant with instructions to pay whatever was needed to get me. The servant eventually bought me for eighty pieces of gold but lied to his mistress, saying he had paid one hundred. I knew about the lie, but I kept quiet to protect him.

You see, my children, all the hardship I endured just to protect my brothers from shame. So, I urge you to love one another sincerely and be patient with each other's mistakes. God takes joy in brothers who love and support each other.

When my brothers later came to Egypt, they found that I had secretly returned the money they had given for food. I did not punish them; instead, I comforted them. Even after our father Jacob passed away, I loved my brothers even more. I carried out my father's wishes with great care, and I made sure my brothers never lacked anything.

I treated their children as my own, and my own children served them. Their happiness was my happiness, and their pain was my pain. I shared everything I had with them and never acted as if I was above them, despite my high position. Instead, I lived as their equal.

So, my children, if you follow God's commandments, He will bless and lift you up. If others try to hurt you, do good to them instead and pray for them. God will rescue you from harm.

Look at my life—I was blessed because of humility and patience. I married Asenath, the daughter of an Egyptian priest, and received great wealth. But I remained humble. God continued to bless me, keeping me strong and healthy even in old age. In many ways, I resembled my father, Jacob.

Now, listen to a vision I had. I saw twelve deer eating together. Nine scattered across the earth, while three remained. Then, from Judah came a young woman wearing fine linen. She gave birth to a spotless lamb, and a lion stood beside it. Many wild animals tried to attack the lamb, but it defeated them all. Because of this lamb, both people and angels rejoiced, and the whole earth was filled with joy.

This vision will come true in the future. So, my children, follow God's commandments and honor Levi and Judah, for from them will come the Lamb of God. He will take away the sins of the world and bring salvation to everyone, both Israel and other nations. His kingdom will last forever, unlike mine, which was only temporary.

I know that after my death, the Egyptians will oppress you. But God will bring justice and lead you to the land He promised to our ancestors. When you leave Egypt, take my bones with you. When you do, God's light will be with you, while darkness will remain with the Egyptians.

Bury your mother, Asenath, near Rachel's resting place. After saying these words, Joseph lay down, stretched out his feet, and peacefully passed away at a good old age.

All of Israel mourned for Joseph, and even the Egyptians grieved with them. When the Israelites left Egypt, they carried Joseph's bones and buried him in Hebron, with his ancestors. Joseph lived to be 110 years old.

The Testament of Benjamin

The Twelfth Son of Jacob and Rachel.

Chapter I.

Benjamin, the youngest son of Jacob and Rachel, grew up to be a wise and kind man.

Before he passed away at the age of 125, he gathered his children, kissed them, and shared his final words:

"I was born when my father, Jacob, was very old, just as Isaac was born to Abraham in his old age. Sadly, my mother, Rachel, died giving birth to me, so I never got to drink her milk. Instead, her servant Bilhah nursed me and cared for me as her own child.

For twelve years after Joseph was born, my mother could not have more children. But she prayed to God with all her heart, fasting for twelve days, and He answered her prayers—she became pregnant and gave birth to me. My father had always wanted Rachel to have two sons, and when I was born, he named me Benjamin, meaning 'son of days,' because I was the answer to his prayers.

When I traveled to Egypt and met my brother Joseph, he recognized me and asked, 'What did our brothers tell our father when they sold me?' I answered, 'They dipped your coat in blood and sent it to him, saying, "Look at this and see if it belongs to your son."' Joseph then told me, 'When they took my coat, they sold me to the Ishmaelites. They gave me only a loincloth, whipped me, and made me run. But later, one of the men who beat me was killed by a lion, and the others were terrified.'

So, my children, I urge you to love and obey the Lord, the Creator of heaven and earth. Follow the example of Joseph, who was a good and righteous man. If your heart is focused on doing what is right, you will see things clearly. Love God and be kind to others. Even if evil forces try to harm you, they will not succeed—just as they could not defeat Joseph.

Think about how many people wanted to hurt Joseph, but God protected him. Those who love God and care for others are safe from evil plans. No enemy, whether human or animal, can destroy them because the Lord is their protector.

Joseph even prayed for our father to forgive his brothers for their cruelty. Jacob, deeply moved, embraced Joseph, kissed him, and wept for a long time. Then he spoke of the future, saying, 'Through you, my son, a great prophecy will be fulfilled. A sinless one will be sacrificed for the sake of sinners. His blood will bring salvation to both Israel and other nations. He will defeat evil and those who serve it.'

My children, do you see what happens to a good and righteous person? Follow his example so you, too, can receive rewards in heaven. A good person does not give in to jealousy or hatred. He is kind to everyone, even those who do wrong. If others try to harm him, he responds with goodness, knowing that God is his shield. He treats the righteous as if they were his own family. He is not jealous of the wealthy or envious of those who succeed. Instead, he admires those who are strong and virtuous. He helps the poor, shows compassion to the weak, and praises God with joy.

A kind-hearted person loves others who have a noble spirit as if they were his own soul. If you live this way, even wicked people will treat you with kindness. Your goodness may inspire the unjust to change their ways. Those who are greedy may learn to be generous. When you act righteously, even evil spirits will flee from you, and wild animals will fear you. Darkness cannot overpower a person filled with goodness and light.

If someone harms a righteous man, they will regret it because a righteous man does not seek revenge. Even when betrayed, he prays for the one who wronged him. He may suffer for a time, but in the end, he will be lifted up—just like Joseph. A good man does not fall for the tricks of evil, because the angel of peace guides him. He does not focus on worldly riches or chase after pleasure. He does not harm others or desire things that belong to them. His greatest treasure is the Lord, and he finds joy in Him alone.

A good heart does not waver between kindness and cruelty, truth and lies, or love and hatred. It is pure and steady, loving all people equally. Such a person does not seek human praise or fear human rejection, for God is their true home, and His light fills their soul.

So, my children, always strive to have good and noble hearts. Obey the Lord's commandments with all your strength. Stay away from dishonesty, hatred, and falsehood. Instead, live with purity and love for everyone. By doing so, you will reflect God's image, and His peace will always be with you.

A righteous person keeps his mind pure so that neither people nor God can find fault with him. In contrast, evil people are full of lies and deceit, always changing their minds and never acting with honesty.

This is why, my children, I urge you to stay far away from evil. Those who follow wickedness may feel powerful for a time, but it will only lead to destruction. It brings seven great troubles: first, it corrupts the mind; then it leads to violence, ruin, suffering, exile, hunger, fear, and ultimately, complete destruction.

This is why God punished Cain seven times over, for he was guilty of great evil. Every hundred years, God sent a plague upon him. His suffering began when he was two hundred years old, and by the time he reached nine hundred, his life came to an end.

This was God's judgment for Cain's sin against his brother Abel. In the same way, Lamech, who committed similar sins, was punished seventy times seven. Let this be a lesson: those who hold onto jealousy and hatred, like Cain did, will face God's judgment forever."

Chapter II.

The third verse gives a clear and down-to-earth example of how the ancient patriarchs spoke.

Now, my children, I encourage you to stay away from evil actions, jealousy, and hatred toward your brothers. Instead, fill your hearts with goodness and love. Let love guide your thoughts and actions in everything you do.

A person with a pure heart and a mind full of love will not look at a woman with lustful thoughts. Such a person remains pure, for God's Spirit lives within them. Just like the sun can shine on dirt without being stained but instead dries it up and removes the bad smell, a pure heart stays clean even when surrounded by a sinful world.

According to the words of the righteous Enoch, I know that evil will rise among you. Many will fall into sin, following the ways of Sodom, and they will be destroyed—except for a small group who remain faithful. Many will return to sinful ways with women, and because of this, the kingdom of God will be taken away from them.

Still, the temple of God will remain among you, and in the future, there will be a final temple that will be even more glorious than the first. The twelve tribes will gather there, along with many people from other nations. This will continue until the Most High sends His salvation through His one and only prophet. This prophet will enter the first temple, where He will be rejected and treated with great dishonor. He will be lifted up on a tree, and the temple veil will tear apart. Then, God's Spirit will come upon the Gentiles like fire.

This prophet will rise from the dead and ascend into heaven. I know that He will live humbly on earth, yet rule with great glory in heaven.

When Joseph was in Egypt, I deeply wished to see him. Through the prayers of our father Jacob, God granted me a vision of Joseph's face during the day, showing me exactly how he looked.

After saying these things, he turned to his children and said, "My dear children, my time to leave this world has come. So, live in truth, be honest with one another, and follow the Lord's laws and commandments. These are the most valuable treasures I leave for you. Pass them on to your children, just as Abraham, Isaac, and Jacob passed them down to us.

They taught us to remain faithful to God's commands until the time when the Lord brings salvation to all nations. Then, you will see Enoch, Noah, Shem, Abraham, Isaac, and Jacob rise again in joy and stand at God's right hand.

On that day, we will rise again and lead our tribes in worshiping the King of heaven, who came to earth as a humble man. Those who believe in Him will rejoice with Him.

All people will rise—some to honor and others to shame. The Lord will judge Israel first because, when He came to save them, they did not believe in Him. Then, He will judge the Gentiles who also refused to believe in Him when He walked among them. Israel will be held accountable through the faith of the Gentiles, just as Esau was judged through the Midianites. These deceivers led their own brothers into sin and idolatry, causing them to turn away from God instead of joining those who truly fear the Lord.

But if you, my children, live in holiness and obey God's commandments, we will be together again, and all of Israel will be gathered to the Lord. I will no longer be known as a wild and greedy wolf because of past mistakes, but as a servant of God who provides for those who do good.

In the last days, someone greatly loved by God will rise from the tribes of Judah and Levi. He will carry out God's will and bring new knowledge that will enlighten the Gentiles. Until the end of time, his words and deeds will be remembered like a beautiful song among the Gentiles and their rulers. His life and works will be written in the holy books, and he will remain God's chosen servant forever.

He will walk among the tribes, fulfilling what is missing, just as my father Jacob prophesied. After saying these words, he lay back, stretched out his feet, and peacefully passed away in a calm and beautiful sleep.

His sons honored his last wishes, carrying his body to Hebron and burying him with his ancestors. He lived for a total of one hundred and twenty-five years.

Testament of Job

Chapter 1

One day, when Job was very sick and knew he was about to die, he called his seven sons and three daughters to his side. He said to them:

"Come close, my children, and listen to me. I want to tell you what God has done in my life and everything I've gone through. I am your father, Job.

"You come from a special family. You belong to a chosen line, so don't forget the honor that comes with it. I am a descendant of Esau. My brother is Nahor, and your mother is Dinah. She gave birth to all of you. My first wife passed away along with our ten children in a terrible accident.

"Now let me tell you my story. I was once a very wealthy man living in the East, in a land called Uz. Before God changed my name to Job, I was known as Jobab.

"My hardship began like this: Near my house, people worshiped an idol. They made sacrifices to it and treated it like a god. I saw this often and asked myself, 'Is this really the one who created the heavens, the earth, the seas, and all living things? How can I know the truth?'

"That night, while I was asleep, I heard a voice calling me, 'Jobab! Jobab! Get up, and I'll show you the truth about the one you're searching for.' The voice told me, 'The idol that people worship is not God. It's something Satan created to fool them.'

"When I heard that, I dropped to the ground and prayed, 'Lord, thank you for helping me understand. If this is really Satan's idol, please let me destroy it so I can make this place clean again. I'm the ruler here, and no one can stop me. I want to protect people from being led the wrong way.'

"Then the voice from the fire answered, 'Yes, you can clean this place. But listen carefully. I have a message from God. I am the archangel of the Lord.' I said, 'I'm ready to hear and follow whatever God tells me.'

"The archangel said, 'Here is what God says: If you destroy the idol of Satan, he will get very angry. He will come after you with all his power. He'll cause you great suffering. He'll take your children, your wealth, and everything you have. You will face a lot of pain and hardship.

"But if you stay strong and keep your faith, like an athlete who doesn't give up in a tough race, you will win in the end. God will reward you greatly. People will remember your name for all time. God will give you back more than what you lost—twice as much—so you'll see that He blesses those who stay faithful and do what's right.

"You'll receive a crown that never fades. And when the day comes, you'll rise again to live forever. Then you'll know for sure that the Lord is fair, powerful, and faithful.'

"My children, when I heard all this, I said, 'Because I love God, I'll go through anything, even death. I won't turn away.' Then the angel marked me with his seal and left."

Chapter 2

That night, I woke up and took fifty of my servants with me. We went to the temple where people worshiped an idol, and I destroyed it completely. Afterward, I went back home and told the guards at my door, "Lock the door well. If anyone comes looking for me, don't disturb me. Just say, 'He's busy with something important inside.'"

Satan then came, pretending to be a poor man, and knocked loudly on the door. He told the guard, "Tell Job I want to speak with him."

The guard came in and gave me the message, but I told him I was busy studying and not to let anyone in.

Since that didn't work, Satan went away and came back carrying an old, torn basket. He told the guard, "Ask Job to give me some bread to eat." When I heard this, I told the servant to give him some burnt leftovers and to say, "You're not allowed to eat my bread."

But the guard, embarrassed to hand over burnt bread and not realizing who he really was, gave him some of her own fresh bread instead. Satan took it and, knowing she disobeyed, said to her, "You're a bad servant. Go get the bread your master told you to give me."

The servant felt ashamed and said, "You're right—I didn't follow his instructions." So she went back, got the burnt bread, and handed it to him. She added, "This is what my master said: 'You're not allowed to eat my bread. But I'm still giving it to you so no one can say I refused to feed someone who asked—even an enemy.'"

When Satan heard that, he said to her, "Just like this bread is burned, I'm going to burn Job's body until he looks just like this."

I answered, "Do whatever you want. Carry out your plans. I'm ready to handle whatever you bring against me."

After that, Satan left. He went up to the highest heaven and got permission from God to take everything I had. As soon as he was given that power, he took away all of my wealth.

Chapter 3

I owned 130,000 sheep, and I set aside 7,000 of them to make clothes for orphans, widows, the sick, and anyone in need. I also had 800 dogs to guard my sheep and another 200 dogs to guard my house.

I had nine mills that made food for the whole city, and I owned ships that carried supplies. I sent those supplies to towns and villages nearby to help the sick and poor. I also had 340,000 donkeys that traveled from place to place. Out of those, I picked 500 and sold their young. I gave all the money to help people who were struggling.

People came from all over to ask for help. My house had four doors, each with a watchman. Their job was to look for anyone needing help. If I was sitting at one door, people could come in through another, take what they needed, and leave quietly.

I always kept 30 tables filled with food for travelers and 12 more tables for widows. Anyone who came for help found food, and I never sent anyone away hungry.

I had 3,500 teams of oxen. I chose 500 of them to plow the fields. Anyone who wanted to work the land could do so, and whatever they harvested, I gave to the poor.

I ran 50 bakeries that made bread for the poor. I had servants who served the food. Even strangers, after seeing my kindness, volunteered to help. Some of them were in hard times and asked, "Can you lend us money to buy goods to sell in big cities? We'll give whatever extra we earn to the poor and return your money afterward."

I was happy to help. I gave them what they asked for and only requested a written promise—they didn't need to give me anything else as proof.

They went out and helped others with what they earned. But sometimes they lost their goods while traveling, or they were robbed. When that happened, they came back and said, "Please give us more time. We want to pay you back."

I felt compassion for them. I read their promises out loud, then tore them up and said, "I won't take back anything that was meant to help the poor." So I never asked them to repay me.

Sometimes, someone would come and say happily, "I don't want any pay. I just want to help serve the poor." If he agreed to work, I still gave him his full pay. And if he didn't want to take it, I insisted, saying, "You've worked hard, and you deserve this."

I never delayed anyone's pay. I made sure they got it the same day. The people who milked the cows and sheep would call out to others walking by, telling them to take some. We had so much milk that it turned into butter out in the open, near the roads and hills. The animals rested peacefully by the rocks after giving birth.

My workers got tired from cutting meat into small portions for the widows and the poor. Sometimes they complained, saying, "If only we could eat some of his meat," even though I was generous with them.

I also had six harps, a lyre, and a ten-stringed instrument. I played them during the day. After the widows finished their meals, they would sing back in response. I used music to help them remember and praise God.

When my female workers were upset or worn out, I would pick up the instruments myself and play for them—just like they would if they were on duty. That way, they could rest and feel encouraged.

Chapter 4

My children took turns serving meals each day. They ate together with their three sisters, starting with the oldest brother. It was like a small feast every day.

Each morning, I got up early and offered sacrifices for their sins—fifty rams and nineteen sheep. Whatever meat was left over, I gave to the poor. I told the people, "Take this food and pray for my children. Maybe they've sinned without realizing it—maybe they've said something proud like, 'We're rich and don't need to help the poor.' If they've spoken like that with arrogance, they might have angered God. Pride like that is something God really hates."

I also brought oxen to the altar and said to the priest, "Please let these be a prayer for my children. May they never think badly about God in their hearts."

While I was living this way, doing good as much as I could, Satan couldn't stand it. He asked God for permission to test me, and then came after me in a cruel way.

First, he burned all my sheep. Then he went after my camels, cattle, and every herd I had. Some animals were taken by enemies—even by people I had helped before. My shepherds came and told me what happened.

When I heard the news, I praised God. I didn't curse or blame Him.

When Satan saw I stayed strong, he made another plan. This time, he pretended to be the king of Persia. He attacked my city and took everyone away. Then he told them lies, saying proudly, "This man Job took everything for himself. He even destroyed God's temple. Now I will do the same to him."

He added, "Let's go rob the rest of what's in his house." But some people said, "He still has seven sons and three daughters. Be careful—they might run away, become powerful, and come back to fight us."

But Satan answered, "Don't worry. I already burned his animals and took his wealth. Now I'm going to kill his children."

Then he went and collapsed the house on top of them, killing all of them.

The people in my city saw that his words had come true. They turned against me, stormed my house, and stole everything. I watched with my own eyes as everything I had was taken. Strangers—people with no manners or honor—sat at my table and used my furniture, and I couldn't say a word to stop them.

I felt completely worn out, like a woman in labor overwhelmed by pain. But I remembered what the angel of the Lord had told me—that this would happen.

I felt like someone on a ship in a stormy sea. When the cargo is too heavy and the waves are rough, sometimes you have to throw things overboard just to keep the ship from sinking. I thought, "Let everything go if I can just make it through this and reach safety. If I survive, that will be my reward."

Then another messenger came and told me that my children were gone. I was filled with grief and fear. I tore my clothes and cried out, "The Lord gave, and the Lord has taken away. Whatever the Lord thinks is best, let it be done. May His name be praised."

Chapter 5

When Satan saw that he couldn't break my spirit, he went to ask God for permission to hurt my body. He couldn't stand how patient I was. God allowed him to test me physically but made it clear that he wasn't allowed to touch my soul.

One day, as I sat mourning the loss of my children, Satan came at me like a violent storm. He knocked over my throne and threw me to the ground. I lay there for three hours. Then, he struck me with painful sores from the top of my head to the bottom of my feet.

I was so sick and ashamed that I left the city and sat on a pile of trash. My skin was full of sores, and my body was covered in pus and worms. When a worm fell off my skin, I gently put it back and said, "Stay where you were placed until the one who sent you tells you to leave."

I stayed like that for seven years, sitting on a garbage heap outside the city, covered in sickness.

Even though I was suffering, I saw something amazing with my own eyes: my children being carried to heaven by angels.

Then I saw my wife—who had once lived in luxury, protected by guards—working like a servant, carrying water for a poor man just to earn a little bread to bring to me. It broke my heart. I thought, "How can those proud city leaders—people I wouldn't even compare to my shepherd dogs—now treat my wife like a slave?"

But seeing her gave me strength again.

Later, even that little bit of bread wasn't given freely anymore. She was only allowed enough for herself. Still, she shared what little she had with me. She cried, "What misery! He can't even eat bread anymore, and he's too weak to go to the market to beg for food."

Satan saw this and disguised himself as a bread seller. My wife ran into him by chance and asked him for bread, thinking he was just an ordinary man. Satan said, "If you want bread, you have to pay for it."

She replied, "Where would I get money? Don't you know the troubles I've been through? If you have any mercy, please show it."

But he said, "If you didn't deserve all this, it wouldn't be happening to you. If you have no money, give me your hair. I'll trade it for three loaves of bread—enough to last for three days."

She thought to herself, "What's my hair worth compared to my husband starving to death?" After thinking it over, she agreed. "Fine," she said. "Cut off my hair."

So Satan pulled out scissors and cut off her hair in front of everyone. Then he gave her three loaves of bread.

She took the bread and brought it to me. But Satan followed her on the road, hiding from sight and filling her heart with sorrow and fear.

Chapter 6

One day, my wife came to me crying loudly. Through her tears, she said, "Job! How much longer will you sit out here on this pile of trash, waiting for something to change? I've been going from place to place, working like a servant just to survive. People don't even remember your name anymore.

"Our children, the ones I carried and raised with so much love—they're gone. All my struggles feel meaningless now. And you, covered in sores and worms, sleep out here in the cold every night.

"I've gone through so much just to bring you a little food. I'm not allowed to take extra anymore. I barely have enough for myself, but I still share it with you because I can't bear to see you hungry. That's why I went to the market, even though it was humiliating.

"When I asked for bread, the seller said, 'If you don't have money, give me your hair. I'll give you three loaves so you can survive for a few days.'

"I was desperate, so I said, 'Go ahead, cut it off.' He pulled out scissors and cut my hair right there in the middle of the market while everyone stared.

"People whispered, 'Is that really Sitis, Job's wife? She used to live in a grand house with fancy curtains and guards at the doors. Now she's trading her hair for food!'

"Others said, 'She used to send camels full of supplies to help the poor. Now she's begging!'

'She once kept tables filled with food for strangers and the hungry. Now she's giving up her hair for a few loaves!'

'She once washed her feet in gold and silver bowls. Now she walks barefoot, asking for bread!'

'She wore fine clothes stitched with gold. Now she's giving away her hair just to eat!'

'She used to rest on beds made of silver and gold. Now she trades what little she has left just to survive.'

"Job, after hearing all that, I only have one thing left to say: I'm broken. Please, eat this bread, say something against God, and just let yourself die. I'd rather die myself than go on like this."

But I told her, "I've been sick for seven years. My body's full of sores, and worms eat my flesh. But my heart hasn't given up. And now you're asking me to turn on God?

"No. I'll keep going through all this, even if everything we had is gone. We must stay strong. Do you really want us to turn away from God and follow evil?

"Don't you remember all the blessings we had? If God gave us good things, shouldn't we also accept the bad and trust that He'll show us mercy again?

"Can't you see? It's Satan trying to confuse you and use you to get to me."

Then I turned to Satan and said, "Why are you hiding behind my wife? Come out and face me yourself. Are you a coward? Fight me directly if you have the courage!"

Satan stepped out from behind my wife and stood in front of me, crying. He said, "Job, I give up. You're just a weak human, and I'm a spirit. You're covered in disease, but I'm the one losing this fight.

"It's like I'm a wrestler who got completely beaten. You're lying there sick and broken, but you still speak like a champion. You've won, Job. I admit defeat."

Then he left, humiliated.

So, my children, always stay strong during hard times. A strong heart is more powerful than anything else.

Chapter 7

One day, kings from nearby lands heard about what had happened to me. They each traveled from their homes to visit and comfort me. When they arrived and saw my condition, they cried out loudly and tore their clothes in sorrow. Then they bowed to the ground and sat beside me without saying a word for seven full days and nights.

There were four of them: Eliphaz, king of Teman; Bildad; Zophar; and Elihu. While sitting with me, they quietly spoke to one another about all I had lost.

They remembered the first time they visited me, back when I had shown them my collection of rare and precious stones. They were amazed and said, "Even if all three of us combined everything we own, it wouldn't compare to Jobab's treasure. He's the most honored man in the East."

But now, as they returned to the land of Uz to see me, they asked the townspeople, "Where is Jobab, the ruler of this land?" The people replied, "He's been sitting outside the city on a trash heap for seven years."

The kings asked about my wealth, and the people told them everything—how I had lost it all. So the kings left the city with the citizens and came to find me. When they saw me, they couldn't believe it was really me.

"This can't be Jobab," they said, shocked. But Eliphaz, the king of Teman, said, "Let's get closer and see for ourselves."

As they approached, I recognized them and began to weep. I threw dirt on my head and bowed low, letting them know it was truly me. When they saw this, they collapsed to the ground, overcome with emotion. For three hours, they lay there, as if they were lifeless.

Then they stood up and said to each other, "We can't believe this is Jobab." For the next seven days, they kept asking people about me, trying to understand how someone so generous could lose everything. They said, "Didn't he give food and gifts to cities and towns, even more than what he gave from his own home? How could someone like that end up in such misery?"

After a week, Elihu said, "Let's take a closer look and make sure this is really him."

They were still a little distance away from me, and because I smelled so bad, they carried perfumes to help them get closer. Their soldiers went ahead, spreading sweet-smelling incense all around. After three hours of doing this, they finally came near enough to speak.

Then Eliphaz said, "Is it really you, Job? Are you the same king we once knew? The one who shone as brightly as the sun in the day and glowed like the stars at night?"

I said, "Yes, it's me."

They all burst into tears and sang a royal mourning song. Even their soldiers joined them in sorrow.

Then Eliphaz continued, "Weren't you the one who gave 7,000 sheep to clothe the poor? Where is your throne now?

"Didn't you give 3,000 oxen to help plow fields for those in need? Where is your greatness now?

"You once had golden couches—now you sit on a trash heap. What happened?

"You had 60 tables always ready with food for the poor. You owned incense burners filled with rare perfumes. And now you sit here smelling terrible. What happened?

"You used to have golden lampstands with silver bases. Now you long just to see moonlight.

"You had oils made with the finest spices. Now people can hardly stand to be near you.

"You laughed at the foolishness of the wicked. Now people laugh at you. Where did all your glory go?"

Eliphaz wept for a long time, and the other kings cried with him. The noise was so great that it felt like a public mourning. Then I spoke:

"Be still, and I'll tell you about my true throne and the glory that can't be taken away. My glory will never end. The world and everything in it will pass away. Those who chase after it will fall. But my throne is in heaven, and its beauty is beside the Savior.

"My throne belongs with the lives of those who live purely, and its glory never fades. Rivers on earth will dry up, and the proud will fall. But the rivers that run around my throne will never stop flowing—they are full of strength.

Kings will die. Rulers will disappear. Their power and fame are like shadows in a mirror. But my kingdom will last forever. Its beauty and glory ride with the chariot of my Father in heaven."

Chapter 8

When I finished speaking, Eliphaz got upset and said to the others, "Why did we even come here with our armies to comfort him? He's insulting us now! Just look at him—he's sitting in misery, covered in sores and worms, and yet he dares to say, 'Kingdoms and kings will fall, but my kingdom will last forever.'"

Then Eliphaz stood up, clearly angry. "I'm leaving," he said. "We came to bring comfort, but he's acting like we've come to fight him."

But Bildad held him back and said, "That's not the right way to talk to someone who's suffering. Job's been through so many terrible things. Even we, who are healthy, didn't dare come near him without using strong perfumes to block the smell. Have you already forgotten all that?

"Let's be kind. Let's try to understand what caused this. It makes sense that someone who remembers better days might feel like he's losing his mind. Who wouldn't be confused and overwhelmed after falling from such a high place into such deep pain?

"I'm going to speak with him myself and find out what's really going on."

So Bildad walked closer to me and said, "Are you really Job? Is your heart still strong and steady?"

I answered, "I never held tightly to things on earth, because everything here changes. But my heart is steady because it's fixed on heaven, and nothing there falls apart."

Then Bildad said, "Yes, the earth changes with the seasons—sometimes peaceful, sometimes full of conflict. But we've heard heaven is always calm and steady.

"So, are you really at peace inside? Let me ask you something. If you can answer well, then I'll ask more. If your answers show wisdom, we'll know your heart hasn't turned bitter or confused."

He asked, "What do you put your hope in?"

I said, "I hope in the living God."

Then he asked, "Who took away everything you owned? Who caused you all this suffering?"

I replied, "God did."

He said, "If you still trust in God, how can He be fair if He let all of this happen to you? Why would God take away your health and wealth if you truly served Him? A good king doesn't treat his loyal soldiers like that."

I answered, "No one can fully understand God's deep wisdom. Who are we to say He's wrong?"

Bildad replied, "Then explain this, Job. If your mind is still clear, tell me with wisdom: Why does the sun always rise in the east and set in the west? Why does it do the same thing every day?"

I said, "Why should I try to explain the secrets of God? Should I make wild guesses about things that belong only to the Master of the universe? No, never. Who are we to question the mysteries of heaven when we ourselves are just dust and ashes?

"But if you want proof that my heart and mind are still clear, let me ask you something. Food goes into the stomach, and water goes in through the mouth. They both travel down the same throat, but once inside, they're separated before leaving the body. Who makes that happen?"

Bildad said, "I don't know."

And I replied, "If you can't even explain what happens inside your own body, how can you understand the way heaven works?"

Then Zophar jumped in and said, "We're not asking to debate mysteries. We just want to know if your mind is still strong—and from what we've seen, it is. So tell us what we can do for you. We brought the best doctors from three different kings. If you want, they can try to heal you."

I answered, "My healing and strength won't come from them. It will come only from God, who created even the doctors."

Chapter 9

While I was still talking with the kings, my wife, Sitis, came running toward us. She was wearing torn, ragged clothes because she had been working as a servant. Her boss had warned her not to leave, worried the kings might see her and take her away. But she came anyway, because she was desperate.

She fell to the ground at the kings' feet, crying, "Eliphaz, and all of you—please remember who I used to be. Look at me now. Look at how I've changed. Just look at what I'm wearing."

The kings started crying too. They were speechless. Eliphaz took off his royal robe and handed it to her so she could cover herself.

Then Sitis pleaded, "Please, kind sirs, I beg you—ask your soldiers to dig through the ruins of our house. It fell down on top of our children. Maybe they can find their bones, so we can at least give them a proper burial.

"We've lost everything, and we don't have the strength to do it ourselves. I just want to see my children's bones one last time.

"Am I worse than a wild animal? Even wild mothers care about their babies. But all ten of my children died in one day, and I couldn't even bury a single one."

The kings agreed and ordered their men to dig through the rubble. But I stopped them.

"Don't waste your time," I said. "You won't find them. My children are safe in the care of their Creator."

The kings looked at each other, confused. "He must be losing his mind," they said. "We're offering to help find his children, and he says they're with God. He needs to prove it."

So I said, "Lift me up so I can stand." They held my arms and helped me rise to my feet.

Standing up, I first praised God. Then I prayed and said, "Look to the East."

They turned their heads—and saw my children wearing shining crowns, standing in glory near the King of Heaven.

When Sitis saw this, she dropped to the ground and worshiped God. She said, "Now I know that the Lord still remembers me."

That evening, she returned to the city and went back to the home of the man she worked for. She laid down near the animals' feeding trough and passed away from exhaustion.

The next morning, her cruel master looked for her but couldn't find her. He searched and finally saw her lifeless body lying near the animals. The animals around her were crying loudly, as if they were mourning her death.

Everyone who saw her wept, and the sound of their grief spread through the whole city. They gently wrapped her body and buried her near the ruins of our home, where our children had died.

The poor people of the city mourned her deeply. They said, "Look at Sitis—no woman was ever as noble or kind as she was. But even she didn't get the kind of grave she deserved."

A special mourning song was written for her and kept in the records.

Chapter 10

Eliphaz and his friends were stunned by everything that had happened to me. They stayed with me and talked for twenty-seven days straight. The whole time, they insisted I must have sinned badly and that I deserved all this suffering. They said there was no hope for me. But I didn't back down—I argued with them, and we kept debating.

Eventually, they got frustrated and wanted to leave angrily. That's when Elihu stepped in and asked them to wait a little longer so he could speak. He said, "You've let Job claim he's innocent for days now, and I can't take it anymore. At first, I felt sorry for him because of everything he lost. But now he's acting proud, talking like he has a throne in heaven. I'll explain what's really going on."

Then Elihu, influenced by something not from God, spoke harshly. His words were so cruel they were written down as a warning for others. After he finished, God appeared to me in a storm and thick clouds. He spoke, correcting Elihu and revealing that Elihu wasn't speaking with wisdom, but like a wild, foolish creature.

Once God finished talking to me, He turned to Eliphaz and said, "You and your friends did wrong. You didn't speak the truth about my servant Job. So go to him and ask him to offer a sacrifice for you. If it weren't for him, I would have destroyed you."

They brought everything needed for the offering, and I made the
sacrifice on their behalf. God accepted it and forgave them.

When Eliphaz, Bildad, and Zophar saw that God had forgiven
them through me—but had not forgiven Elihu—they sang a song of
praise. Their soldiers joined in while standing near the altar. Eliphaz
led the hymn, saying:

"Our sins are gone,
our mistakes are erased.
But Elihu, the evil one,
won't be remembered among the living.
His light is gone,
his flame has burned out.
His honor has vanished;
he belongs to the darkness, not the light.
The guardians of the dark
will be his only prize.
His kingdom is lost,
his throne has crumbled,
his pride is buried deep in the grave.
He loved the image of the serpent
and chased after the poison of dragons.
His heart and his words
were full of deadly poison.
He didn't honor or respect the Lord,
and he hated those God chose.
So God turned His back on him,
and the holy ones left him.
His heart is cold,
his words are poisonous.
The Lord is just;
His judgments are true.
He doesn't play favorites
and treats everyone fairly.

Look, the Lord is coming!
The holy ones are ready!
Crowns and rewards
are waiting for them.
Let the faithful celebrate
and be filled with joy,
because their reward is on the way."
Then the chorus answered:
"Our sins are forgiven,
our wrongs are gone,
but Elihu is forgotten among the living."

After the hymn ended, we all went back to the city and returned to our homes.

The people welcomed me with a big feast. They were thankful to God and full of joy. All my old friends came back to see me again.

Those who had known me during my days of wealth and honor looked around and asked, "What are these three things we see now?"

Chapter 11

I wanted to start helping the poor again, so I asked my friends, "Each of you, please give me a lamb to make clothes for the poor who have nothing to wear, and four silver or gold coins."

Then God blessed the little I still had. In just a few days, I became wealthy again. I got back all my animals, goods, and riches—everything I had lost was returned to me, but doubled.

Later, I married your mother and became the father of you ten, to replace the ten children I had lost.

Now, my children, listen carefully—my time is almost up, and you will carry on after me.

Never turn away from God. Be kind to the poor. Don't ignore people who are weak. And don't marry people from foreign lands.

I will now divide everything I own among you so that each of you can manage your own share and use it for good.

So I gathered all my belongings and gave them to my seven sons. But I didn't give any of my possessions to my daughters.

They asked me, "Father, aren't we your children too? Why didn't you give us anything?"

I replied, "Don't be upset, my daughters. I haven't forgotten you. I've saved something even better for you—something greater than what your brothers received."

Then I called for my daughter named Day (Yemima) and said, "Take this special ring that also works as a key, go to the treasure room, and bring me the golden box so I can give you your gift."

She did as I asked, brought the box, and I opened it. Inside were three glowing belts, made of light and beauty beyond anything on earth. They shimmered like sunlight and didn't look like anything made by people.

I gave one to each daughter and said, "Wrap these belts around you. As long as you wear them, they will surround you with goodness for the rest of your life."

Then my daughter Kassia asked, "Is this really the gift you said was better than our brothers'? How are we supposed to live on this?"

I told her, "These belts don't just take care of your needs—they lead you to a better life in heaven. Don't you understand their value? Listen carefully.

"When the Lord chose to show mercy to me and healed me from the diseases and worms that covered my body, He gave me these three belts. He said, 'Get ready like a man—I'm going to ask you questions, and you must answer.' I tied them around my waist, and the worms left me. My sickness disappeared. My body became strong again, as if I had never been sick.

"And even the pain in my heart vanished. After that, the Lord showed me everything—what had happened, and what would happen in the future.

"So now, my children, as long as you keep these belts, no evil will trick you. No bad thoughts will fill your minds. These are gifts from the Lord that protect you.

"Put them on before I die, so you can see the angels that will come when I leave this world. You'll witness God's power with your own eyes."

Then Yemima, my daughter named Day, put on her belt. Just as I said, her spirit changed. She no longer cared about anything on earth. She started singing like an angel and praised God in a voice like theirs, dancing joyfully as she worshipped.

Next, Kassia put on her belt. Her heart changed too—she lost all desire for the things of the world. Her voice took on the language of the heavenly rulers, and she sang songs of praise about the beauty and wonder of heaven. Anyone who wants to understand how heaven works can learn from Kassia's hymns.

Finally, my daughter Amalthea's Horn (Keren Happukh) put on her belt. Her voice also changed, speaking in the language of the angels known as Cherubim. She praised the Lord of the heavenly powers and lifted up His glory.

Anyone who wants to follow and understand the "Glory of the Father" can find that path in the prayers of Amalthea's Horn.

Chapter 12

After Job's three daughters finished their songs, I, Nahor—his brother—sat beside him while he rested. I listened closely to the beautiful hymns they sang, each one taking turns, filling the room with a peaceful silence. I wrote down everything in this book, except for the sacred songs and signs from God, because those were too holy to record.

Job was lying in bed, still weak from illness, but he wasn't in pain. The special belt he wore had kept him from suffering.

Three days later, Job saw holy angels coming to take his soul. He got up right away and gave a harp to his daughter Day (Yemima), a container of incense to Kassia, and a tambourine to Amalthea's Horn (Keren Happukh), so they could welcome the angels with music.

The daughters played their instruments and sang in the holy language, lifting up their voices to praise God.

Then the One who rides the great heavenly chariot appeared. He kissed Job gently, and only the three daughters could see it.

He took Job's soul by the arm, lifted it up, and placed it on the chariot. Together they rose into the sky and headed toward the East.

Job's body was buried in a tomb, with his daughters leading the way. They wore their glowing belts and continued to sing songs honoring God.

I, Nahor, along with Job's seven sons, the townspeople, the poor, orphans, and the weak, all gathered and mourned deeply, crying out:

"Today we lost the one who gave strength to the weak,
Light to the blind,
A father to the orphans.
He welcomed strangers,
Guided the lost,
Protected the poor,
And stood strong for the widows.
How can we not grieve for such a faithful man of God?"

We mourned so deeply that we didn't want to bury him right away. After three days, we gently placed him in the grave, as if he were only sleeping.

People began to call him "the good one," and his name will be honored forever.

Job left behind seven sons and three daughters. No women on earth were as beautiful as his daughters.

His original name was Jobab, but the Lord called him Job.

Before his suffering, Job lived for 85 years. Afterward, everything he had was given back to him double—including his years. He lived another 170 years, making a total of 255.

He lived long enough to see his great-great-grandchildren.

And it is written that he will rise again with those the Lord brings back to life.

Praise be to our Lord. Amen.

Testament of Moses

I.

In the last year of my life—my 120th year—I, Moses, spoke these words. It was about 2,500 years since the creation of the world, or around 2,700 years by Eastern count, and 400 years after the people left Phoenicia.

We had crossed over to Amman, on the other side of the Jordan. That's when I gave my final message, as written in the book of Deuteronomy.

I called Joshua, son of Nun, a man who had proven faithful to the Lord. He would take over leadership, guiding the people and caring for the sacred tent and everything holy in it.

His job would be to lead the people into the land that God had promised to our ancestors. God had sworn to give that land to them, and now it would be Joshua's duty to carry that out.

I told him, "Be careful to follow every command exactly as you've been told. Do everything with dedication, so you will stay blameless before God."

These were the words of the Lord, the one who created everything for the sake of His chosen people.

He didn't show this plan clearly from the start so that other nations would argue and be confused. That way, their pride would lead them to embarrass themselves through their own debates.

God had chosen me long ago to serve as the go-between for His agreement with His people.

Now, my time has come. I've reached the end of my life, and soon I will join my ancestors.

Take this writing and protect it carefully. I'll give you the sacred books.

Cover them with cedar oil, seal them in clay jars, and place them in the special spot God made at the beginning of creation.

That place will carry His name until the time of repentance—when He visits His people at the end of the age.

II.

The people will enter the land just as God promised their ancestors. When they do, you must bless them and assign each one their share of land.

You will help set up their kingdom and appoint judges to rule over their areas, always doing what is right and fair in the eyes of God.

Five years after entering the land, leaders and kings will rule for eighteen years.

Then, for nineteen years, ten of the tribes will separate from the others.

Only two tribes will remain faithful, and they will move the sacred tent.

God will then build the wall around His tent and the tower of His holy place. The two faithful tribes will live there.

The ten tribes will go their own way, forming their own kingdom.

For twenty years, they'll bring offerings to their own altar.

Seven of them will build walls around their cities. I will protect nine, but four will break their promise to God and disrespect the sacred agreement.

They will even offer their own children as sacrifices to foreign gods and place idols inside the holy tent to worship them.

They'll commit horrible sins in the Lord's house and carve images of animals and many other false gods.

II.

During their disobedience, they'll be taken away by Nebuchadnezzar into captivity.

But while they're in exile, both the divided tribes will come together and pray with one voice to God.

III.

A king from the East will come with his army and take over the land. He will burn down their city and even the holy temple of the Lord. He will take all the sacred items and carry the people away to his own country, including the two tribes.

The two tribes will call out to the ten tribes for help, but they'll be like a starving lioness in a desert, wandering with their children, hungry and thirsty.

They'll cry out, "The Lord is fair and holy. We sinned, and now we've been taken away with you."

The ten tribes will cry when they hear this. They'll answer, "What did we do to you, our brothers? Hasn't this suffering come upon all of Israel?"

Then all the tribes will cry together, praying to God:

"God of Abraham, Isaac, and Jacob, please remember the promise You made to them—the oath You swore by Your own name—that their children would never lose the land You gave them."

They'll remember me that day, saying to each other, "Isn't this what Moses warned us about? The one who suffered so much in Egypt, at the Red Sea, and during forty years in the desert?"

"Yes, he warned us, calling heaven and earth to witness, telling us not to break God's commands. He was the one God chose to give us those laws."

"And now everything he said has come true. We've been taken away just as he said would happen."

They will remain in captivity for about seventy-seven years.

IV.

Then, one person will stand up among them. He will raise his hands, kneel, and pray:

"Lord of everything, King above all, You rule the world. You chose these people to be special to You. You promised to be their God just like You promised their ancestors.

But now they've been taken far from home, to a land full of idols and emptiness.

Please, Lord of heaven, remember them and have mercy."

God will remember His promise to their ancestors and will show mercy again.

He'll inspire a king to feel compassion for them. That king will let them return to their land.

Some of the tribes will go back and rebuild the place meant for them.

The two tribes will stay true to their faith, but they'll be sad and groaning because they can't offer sacrifices to the God of their ancestors.

The ten tribes will grow and spread among the foreign nations during their time of suffering.

When the day of judgment comes close, kings who shared in their evil will also bring punishment.

But even among them, truth will be divided. As it was once said:

"They'll turn away from what's right, and run toward what's wrong. They'll even make the house where they're held captive filthy. They'll worship strange gods."

They'll forget God's truth. Some will even pollute the altar with unworthy offerings—not given by priests, but by slaves born of slaves.

The leaders and teachers during that time will care more about money and favors than about justice. They'll take bribes and judge unfairly.

All across the land where they live, sin will be everywhere. Their judges will act against the Lord and hand out decisions based on money instead of truth.

VI.

Then kings will rise and rule over them, pretending to be priests of the Most High God. But they'll do evil even in the holiest places.

After them will come a proud and wicked king, not from the priestly family. He will judge them harshly.

He'll kill their leaders and bury them in secret so no one knows where they are.

He won't spare anyone—old or young.

Everyone will fear him in their land.

He will rule like the Egyptians once did, punishing them for thirty-four years.

His sons will rule after him, but their time will be shorter.

Then a powerful Western king will come into their territory.

He will defeat them, take them away as captives, burn part of their temple, and crucify some of them around their city.

VII.

After this, time will run out. Suddenly, the next phase will begin. A period known as the "four hours" will come.

During this time, corrupt and wicked leaders will rule. They'll pretend to be good and righteous, but they won't be.

These people will even make their own friends angry. They'll be tricky and dishonest in everything they do, and they'll spend their days focused on eating and celebrating.

They'll be greedy and selfish, taking what belongs to the poor and pretending they're doing it out of kindness. But in truth, they'll be ruining lives.

They'll complain a lot and lie, hiding their true selves so no one can tell what they're really like. From morning to night, they'll be full of sin and wrongdoing.

They'll say things like, "Give us rich food and fine things! Let's eat, drink, and live large—we're important people!"

Their actions and thoughts will be filthy. Their mouths will speak proud and terrible things.

And they'll even say, "Don't come near me—you might make me unclean just by standing too close."

VIII.

Then, a terrible judgment will come upon them. It will be worse than anything the land has ever seen since the beginning of time.

God will raise up a powerful ruler—the king of all earthly kings—who will bring punishment.

He'll crucify those who stay true to their traditions. He'll torture those who turn away from them and throw many into prison. Their wives will be taken and given to outsiders.

Their sons will be harmed in ways meant to erase their identity.

Some will be tortured with fire, swords, and cruel beatings. They'll be forced to carry idols in public, even though these idols are evil.

Their captors will push them into secret places and force them, with whips and prods, to speak against their own faith. They'll be made to insult the sacred word, mock their own laws, and disrespect what they once held dear at the altar.

IX.

During the rule of a harsh leader, a man from the tribe of Levi named Taxo will rise up. He will have seven sons, and he will say to them,

"My sons, look at what's happening. Another cruel punishment, worse than the first, has fallen on our people.

Think about it—has any other nation who disobeyed God ever suffered as much as we have?

Now listen to me. You know that our parents and grandparents never turned away from God or broke His commands. That has always been our strength.

So let's do something strong and faithful.

Let's fast for three days. Then, on the fourth day, let's go into the cave out in the field and stay there.

We'll die there instead of breaking the commands of the Lord, the God of our ancestors.

If we do this and die, the Lord will see our faith, and He will bring justice for our blood."

X.

Then God's kingdom will appear across the entire world. The devil will be destroyed, and sorrow will disappear with him.

The hands of the angel in heaven will be filled with power, and he will punish the enemies of God's people.

The Holy One will rise from His throne and come down from His holy place. He will come with anger to protect His children.

The earth will shake all over. Tall mountains will crumble and shake. Valleys will collapse.

The sun will go dark. The moon will stop shining and turn to blood. Stars will move out of place.

The sea will dry up and drop into deep pits. Water springs will stop flowing. Rivers will tremble.

All of this will happen because the Almighty God, the Eternal One, will show Himself to punish the nations and destroy their idols.

Then, Israel—you'll be filled with joy. You'll rise like an eagle and soar. Your days of sadness will be over.

God will lift you up and bring you to the stars, to His own home in heaven.

From there, you'll look down and see your enemies on the earth.

You'll recognize them and be glad. You'll thank God and praise your Creator.

Now, Joshua son of Nun, remember these words and keep this book safe.

There will be 250 periods of time from my death until He comes.

This is how the times will pass—until they are complete.

But now I must go to rest with my ancestors.

So be strong, Joshua. God has chosen you to take my place and lead the people under His covenant."

XI.

When Joshua heard all the words Moses had written, he tore his clothes in sorrow and fell at Moses' feet.

Moses comforted him, and they both wept.

Then Joshua said,

"How can you comfort me, Lord Moses, when your words bring such pain? You said you are leaving this people.

Where will you go? What place will be your burial ground?

Who could even carry your body, like they do for other people?

Most people are buried in one place. But you—your resting place will stretch from sunrise to sunset, from south to north. The whole earth will be your tomb.

But once you're gone, who will care for this people?

Who will lead them or show them kindness?

Who will pray for them every day, without stopping, until they reach the land of their ancestors?

How can I guide them, like a father leads his only son, or a woman cares for her daughter, ready to be married, careful not to let the sun touch her skin or her feet touch the dirt?

How can I give them all the food and water they want?

There are 100,000 men now—all because of your prayers, Moses.

What wisdom or understanding do I have to judge them or speak for them before God?

When the kings of the Amorites hear that we're coming, they'll think we have no holy spirit left, no wise and faithful leader like Moses.

They'll say, 'Let's attack them. Their champion is gone. Moses, who prayed day and night with his knees on the ground, is no longer there to speak to God for them.'

They'll say, 'He reminded God of His promises and calmed His anger—but he's gone now. Let's wipe them out.'

What will happen to your people, my Lord Moses?"

XII.

Then Moses encouraged Joshua and placed him in his own seat of leadership. When Joshua finished speaking, he once again fell at Moses' feet.

Moses took his hand and helped him up into the seat in front of him. Then he said,

"Joshua, don't look down on yourself. Stay strong and listen closely to what I'm telling you.

God created all the nations on earth—including us. He knew everything about them and us from the very beginning, even before the world was made. Nothing escapes His notice, no matter how small. He knew everything in advance.

He knew all that would happen in this world, and now it's happening just as He planned.

As for me, God chose me to pray for the people and their sins—to speak up for them before Him.

It wasn't because I was better or stronger than anyone else. It was simply because of God's kindness, mercy, and patience.

So I'm telling you now, Joshua: You won't defeat those nations because our people are especially holy.

Everything in heaven and the earth's foundation was made and approved by God. All of it is sealed under His powerful hand.

Those who follow His commands live well and walk a good path.

But those who ignore Him and break His commands will miss out on the good things promised to them. They'll be punished by other nations in many painful ways.

Even so, God will never completely abandon them. He will not destroy them forever.

Because God, who knew everything from the start, has already gone ahead—and His promise still stands, backed by His own oath."

Testament of Solomon

Introduction

The Testament of Solomon is an ancient text that is not part of the Bible. It is said to be written by King Solomon, the famous ruler of Israel known for his wisdom and for building the First Temple in Jerusalem. Unlike the stories about Solomon in the Bible, this text describes him as someone who had power over demons. According to the story, the archangel Michael gave Solomon a magical ring that allowed him to summon and control spirits. These spirits were connected to different illnesses, temptations, and cosmic forces. Solomon forced them to reveal their names, powers, and weaknesses, including the names of angels who could stop them.

This text is not included in Jewish, Catholic, or Protestant scriptures, but it is important in the study of demons in both Jewish and Christian traditions. It contains ideas from ancient magic, early Christian beliefs, and Babylonian demon stories. Scholars believe it was written between the 1st and 5th centuries CE, with later versions adding more details.

The Testament of Solomon is one of the oldest known books that describes different demons, their abilities, and their roles in the universe. It tells how Solomon used divine power to command demons to help build the Temple, showing his supernatural wisdom and control over both humans and spirits.

Some important ideas in the text include:

- Divine Wisdom and Power – Solomon's power to control demons is a gift from God, proving that real wisdom comes from Him.

- Demons and Angels – The text provides an early list of demons and their weaknesses, often defeated by specific angels. This reflects Jewish and Christian beliefs about exorcism and spiritual battles.
- The Power of God's Name – Many demons are controlled by calling upon God's name, which follows ancient Jewish traditions that believed God's name held great power.
- Solomon's Downfall – The story warns about the dangers of idolatry and sin, showing that even the smartest person can be misled by temptation.

The story is written as if Solomon himself is telling it. It begins with the construction of the Temple in Jerusalem, where a demon named Ornias starts harming one of the workers. Solomon prays for help, and the archangel Michael gives him a magical ring that allows him to control and command demons.

Using this ring, Solomon summons and questions different demons, forcing them to reveal their names, powers, and weaknesses. Some of the most well-known encounters include:

- Ornias, a demon that attacks children, who is defeated with God's seal.
- Beelzebub (Beelzeboul), the prince of demons, who admits he leads people into sin.
- Asmodeus, a demon from the Book of Tobit, who causes trouble for newlyweds.
- Abezithibod, a demon linked to Pharaoh, who claims he made the Egyptian ruler stubborn during the Exodus.
- Ephippas, a spirit from Arabia, who helps Solomon lift a giant stone to finish the Temple.

Solomon uses his ring to command the spirits and make them help build the Temple. But even with his divine power, he is eventually led into sin by a foreign woman. She deceives him into worshiping false gods, which causes him to lose God's favor.

Historical And Religious Background

The Testament of Solomon was likely written in the early centuries CE, possibly in Greek, and influenced by Jewish, Christian, and Greco-Roman traditions. Scholars are unsure of its exact origins, but many believe it was created during a time when Jewish mysticism, Hellenistic magic, and Christian beliefs about demons were blending.

- The Bible – This text expands on Bible stories, especially those in 1 Kings and 2 Chronicles, where Solomon is known for his wisdom. However, instead of showing him only as a wise king, it describes him as a magician who has power over demons.
- The Book of Tobit – The demon Asmodeus, who appears in the Testament of Solomon, also plays a major role in Tobit, where he torments Sarah before being driven away with a fish's liver and heart.
- The Book of Enoch – Like 1 Enoch, this text includes stories of fallen angels and supernatural beings.
- Hellenistic and Babylonian Magic – Many descriptions of demons and their weaknesses are similar to spells and rituals found in ancient Greek and Babylonian traditions.

The Testament of Solomon influenced medieval and Renaissance magic books, including the Key of Solomon, a famous text about mystical practices that was written in the Middle Ages. Even though it is not part of the Bible, it has been studied for its insights into ancient beliefs about demons, angels, and spiritual power.

Today, scholars see it as an important example of early Jewish and Christian mystical writing. It shows how ancient people viewed spiritual battles, divine power, and the supernatural. While it is not a historical record, its impact on religion, folklore, and demonology is clear. Whether read as a legend, mystical story, or religious lesson, it remains a key text in the study of ancient beliefs about the unseen world.

The Testament

The Testament of Solomon tells the story of Solomon, son of David, who was king in Jerusalem. He had the power to control spirits in the air, on the earth, and below the ground. Using this power, he commanded the demons to help build the Temple. The story also explains how these spirits influence people and how angels can defeat them.

Praise to the Lord God, who gave Solomon this power. Glory to Him forever. Amen.

When the Temple of Jerusalem was being built, workers labored daily. One evening, a demon named Ornias appeared and stole half of a young boy's wages and food. He also sucked on the boy's thumb every night, causing him to grow weak and thin. This boy was loved by King Solomon.

One day, Solomon called the boy and asked, "Don't I care for you more than all the other workers? Don't I pay you double and give you extra food? Why do you keep getting thinner every day?"

The boy replied, "Please listen, my king. After we finish working and I go to rest, an evil demon comes and steals half of my pay and my food. He also grabs my right hand and sucks my thumb. Because of this, I feel drained, and my body keeps growing weaker."

When Solomon heard this, he prayed in the Temple, asking God to give him power over the demon. He prayed day and night, and God answered him. The archangel Michael brought Solomon a ring with a special seal carved into it. Michael said, "Take this ring, Solomon, son of David. It is a gift from God. With it, you can trap and command all demons, male and female. They will help you build Jerusalem, but you must always wear this ring. The seal on it is called the Pentalpha."

Solomon was filled with joy and praised God. The next day, he called the boy, handed him the ring, and said, "Take this. When the demon comes to you, throw the ring at his chest and say, 'King Solomon commands you to come!' Then, run straight to me. Do not be afraid of anything the demon says."

The boy took the ring and waited. As usual, Ornias appeared at the same time, burning like fire, ready to steal the boy's wages. But the boy did as Solomon told him—he threw the ring at the demon's chest and called upon the king. Then, he ran to Solomon as fast as he could.

The demon screamed, "Why did you do this to me, child? Take this ring off me, and I will give you all the gold in the world! Please don't take me to Solomon!"

The boy refused to release the demon and said, "As surely as the Lord God of Israel lives, I will not let you go. Come with me." Then he ran happily to King Solomon and said, "I have brought the demon, as you commanded, my lord. He is standing outside the palace gates, crying out loudly and begging. He is offering me silver and gold if I let him go instead of bringing him to you."

When Solomon heard this, he stood up from his throne and went outside to the palace courtyard. There, he saw the demon shaking and afraid. Solomon asked, "Who are you?" The demon replied, "I am called Ornias."

Solomon then asked, "Which zodiac sign are you connected to?" The demon answered, "I belong to the Water-Pourer. I attack people who are filled with desire for noble women, and I strangle them. But if they are not ready to sleep, I change into three different forms. When men desire women, I take the shape of a beautiful woman and visit them in their sleep, playing with them. Then, I grow wings and fly back to the sky. I can also appear as a lion, and I command other demons. I am the child of the archangel Uriel, the power of God."

When Solomon heard the name of the archangel, he prayed and praised God, the ruler of heaven and earth. Then, he placed a seal on Ornias and ordered him to cut stones for the Temple. These stones had been brought from the Arabian Sea. But the demon, afraid of iron tools, pleaded, "King Solomon, please let me go! If you free me, I will bring you all the demons." Since Ornias refused to obey, Solomon prayed to the archangel Uriel for help. At once, Uriel appeared from the heavens.

The angel called the great sea creatures from the deep and cast his power over the demon, forcing him to submit. He ordered Ornias and a powerful demon to cut the stones for the Temple. Seeing this, Solomon praised the God of heaven and earth. He then commanded Ornias to take the ring and bring him the leader of all demons.

Ornias took the ring and went to Beelzebul, the ruler of demons. He said, "Come with me! Solomon is calling you." Beelzebul replied, "Who is this Solomon that you speak of?" Then Ornias threw the ring at Beelzebul's chest, saying, "King Solomon commands you!" Beelzebul let out a loud cry and released a great flame of fire. Then, he rose and followed Ornias to Solomon.

When Solomon saw the ruler of demons, he praised the Lord God, the Creator of heaven and earth. He said, "Blessed are You, Lord Almighty, for giving me wisdom and power over the forces of darkness."

Then, Solomon asked, "Who are you?" The demon answered, "I am Beelzebub, the leader of the demons. All unclean spirits serve me. I am the one who reveals the appearances of each demon." Beelzebul then promised to bring all evil spirits to Solomon in chains. Again, Solomon praised the God of heaven and earth and gave thanks.

Solomon then asked Beelzebul if there were female demons as well. When Beelzebul confirmed that there were, Solomon asked to see one. Beelzebul quickly left and returned with Onoskelis, a demon with the shape of a beautiful woman and smooth, fair skin. She tossed her head proudly as she stood before Solomon.

When she arrived, I asked her, "Who are you?" She replied, "I am called Onoskelis, a spirit connected to the earth. I hide in a golden cave, but I do not stay in one place. Sometimes, I strangle men with a rope, and other times, I creep up their bodies like a worm. I usually stay in cliffs, caves, and deep valleys. But often, I appear as a woman and deceive men, especially those with dark skin, because they unknowingly worship my star. They think they are helping themselves, but they are only feeding my hunger for more evil. They hope I will bring them wealth, and I give them small amounts in return for their devotion."

I then asked her how she was created, and she said, "I was born from a sound that came from a man's waste, echoing through the woods."

I asked, "Which star controls you?" She answered, "I am ruled by the full moon because it moves across everything." Then I asked, "Which angel stops your power?" She replied, "The one who rules through you." Thinking she was mocking me, I ordered a soldier to strike her. But she cried out, "I am under your power, O king, because of the wisdom God has given you and the authority of the angel Joel."

So I commanded her to spin hemp for ropes to be used in building God's Temple. Once I sealed and bound her, she was completely under my control, spinning thread night and day.

Then, I ordered another demon to be brought before me. Immediately, Asmodeus arrived in chains. I asked him, "Who are you?" But he glared at me in anger and snapped, "And who are you?" I answered, "How dare you speak to me this way when you are already punished?" Still filled with rage, he replied, "Why should I answer you? You are only a man. But I was born from the union of an angel and a human woman. No heavenly being speaks to mortals without a reason. My star shines brightly in the sky. Some call it the Wain, and others the child of the dragon. I remain close to it. Do not ask me many questions, for soon, your kingdom will fall. Your rule over us will not last long, and once you are gone, we will again have power over humans. People will worship us as gods, unaware of the names of the angels who control us."

Hearing this, I tightened his chains and ordered him to be whipped with leather straps. Then I demanded that he tell me his name and what he does. He answered, "I am called Asmodeus, and my mission is to cause trouble for newlyweds so that they cannot be happy together. I bring disasters that separate them and destroy the beauty of young women, making their hearts turn cold."

I asked, "Is that all you do?" He replied, "No, I also drive men into obsession and sinful desires. Even when they have wives, I lead them to leave their homes and chase after other women, causing them to sin and commit terrible crimes."

I commanded him in the name of the Lord, saying, "Fear God, Asmodeus, and tell me which angel stops you." He answered, "Raphael, the archangel who stands before God's throne. Also, the smoke from a burning fish liver and gall drives me away." I asked, "Do not hide anything from me. I am Solomon, son of David, King of Israel. Tell me the name of this fish you fear." He said, "It is called Glanos and lives in the rivers of Assyria. That is why I often roam around those areas."

I then asked, "Is there anything else I should know about you, Asmodeus?" He replied, "God, who has bound me with this unbreakable seal, knows that everything I have told you is true. Please, King Solomon, do not send me into the water!" But I smiled and said, "As surely as the Lord God of my ancestors lives, I will make you wear iron chains. You will also be forced to make clay bricks for the Temple, mixing the mud with your feet." I ordered that he be given ten large water jars to carry as punishment.

The demon groaned in agony but obeyed my commands. I did this because I knew Asmodeus could see the future. Then, I praised God for giving me wisdom. I took the liver and gall of the fish and tied them to the end of a reed. I burned them over Asmodeus, weakening his great strength and stopping his evil power.

I called Beelzebul, the prince of demons, and made him sit on an honored seat. I asked, "Why are you alone, ruler of demons?" He replied, "I am the last of the angels who came down from heaven. I was once a high-ranking angel, but now I rule over those trapped in the underworld. I also have a son who lives in the Red Sea. From time to time, he returns to me and tells me what he has done, and I guide him."

I then asked, "What is your role?" He answered, "I destroy kings and work with foreign rulers. I send my demons to deceive people so they will believe in false things and be lost. I tempt God's faithful followers, including priests, leading them to sin, spread false teachings, and commit evil acts. I cause jealousy, hatred, war, and many other terrible things. I seek to ruin the world."

I said, "Bring me your son from the Red Sea." But he refused, saying, "I won't bring him to you, but another demon named Ephippas will come to me, and I will send him to bring my son." I asked, "Why is your son in the sea, and what is his name?" He answered, "I won't tell you, but he will come if you command him, and he will tell you himself."

I then asked, "Which angel has the power to stop you?" Beelzebul replied, "The mighty name of God, which the Hebrews call by numbers adding up to 644, and the Greeks call Emmanuel. If a Roman calls upon the name Eleéth, I am forced to flee immediately."

Hearing this, I was amazed. I ordered him to cut Theban marble stones. As he worked, the other demons screamed and howled in distress because their ruler, Beelzebul, was being forced to obey me.

I then asked him, "If you want relief from your suffering, tell me about the things in heaven." Beelzebul answered, "If you burn incense, sea bulbs, nard, and saffron, and light seven lamps at dawn, you will strengthen your house. If you do this while the sun rises, you will see heavenly dragons winding around and pulling the sun's chariot."

I rebuked him and said, "Enough! Keep cutting the marble as I commanded." Then I praised God and summoned another demon.

A strange spirit appeared before me. His face was high up in the air, but the rest of his body curled like a snail. He burst through my guards and stirred up a great cloud of dust, throwing it into the sky before letting it fall back to the ground to frighten us. Then he asked me what questions I had for him. I spat on the ground, sealed the spot with the ring of God, and immediately, the dust storm stopped. I then asked, "Who are you, O wind?" He stirred up more dust and replied, "What do you want, King Solomon?" I answered, "Tell me your name, for I have been given wisdom from God to see through your tricks."

The demon answered, "I am the spirit of ashes, called Tephras." I asked, "What do you do?" He said, "I bring darkness to people and set fields on fire. I destroy homes, especially in the summer. But I also hide in walls, waiting for the right moment to strike. I come from a powerful source, and my strength is great."

I asked, "Which star rules over you?" He answered, "I live at the tip of the moon's horn when it appears in the south. I was commanded to control the third-day fever, which is why people pray to it, using the names Bultala, Thallal, and Melchal to ask for healing."

I then asked, "When you cause harm, who helps you?" He answered, "An angel controls me, the same one who calms the third-day fever." I demanded, "Tell me the angel's name!" He said, "It is Azael." So I summoned the archangel Azael, sealed the demon, and commanded him to lift heavy stones and carry them up to the workers building the Temple. He had no choice but to obey.

Again, I praised God for giving me this power and called forth another demon. This time, seven spirits appeared before me. They were female, bound together, and looked beautiful. I asked, "Who are you?" They spoke in unison, saying, "We are the seven spirits of darkness."

The first said, "I bring lies and trick people."

The second said, "I cause arguments and division."

The third said, "I create conflict and war."

The fourth said, "I fill hearts with jealousy."

The fifth said, "I make people crave control over others."

The sixth said, "I lead people into making mistakes."

The seventh said, "I am the most dangerous of all. We are seven spirits, moving together like faint stars in the sky. Sometimes we stay in Lydia, other times in Olympus, or on a high mountain."

Solomon questioned each spirit one by one.

The first said, "I bring lies and deception. I trick people and cause confusion. But the angel Lamechalal stops me."

The second said, "I create arguments and conflict. I bring weapons and destruction wherever I go. But the angel Baruchiachel stops me."

The third said, "I cause war and make peaceful people turn against each other. But the angel Marmarath keeps me from doing more harm."

The fourth said, "I make people lose self-control. I divide families, separate husbands from wives, and turn children against their parents. But the angel Balthial stops me."

The fifth said, "I give power to tyrants and help rebels overthrow kings. But the angel Asteraôth weakens my influence."

The sixth said, "I bring confusion and lead people away from what is right. I trick them into doing things that go against God. I have misled even you, Solomon. But the angel Uriel stops me."

The seventh said, "I am the worst of all. I bring destruction and cause people to fall into darkness. Only the locust will release me, for it is destined to play a role in your downfall. A wise person would never come near me."

Solomon listened to them all and sealed them with his ring. Since they were strong, he made them dig the foundation of the Temple. The demons groaned in protest, but they obeyed.

Afterward, Solomon called for another demon, and one appeared with a human body but no head. Solomon asked, "Who are you?"

The demon answered, "I am Envy. I crave what others have. I want a head like yours, but I can never be satisfied."

Solomon sealed the demon with his ring, making him cry out in distress. "I see through my senses, not with eyes. I am nothing but a voice. I take over the voices of those who cannot speak. I also haunt crossroads, harming people. I grab their heads and cut them off, trying to make them my own."

Solomon asked, "How do you create fire?"

The demon answered, "It comes from the morning star. People pray to it and light fires in its name, not knowing that it feeds my power."

Solomon demanded, "Tell me the name of this star!"

The demon refused. "If I speak its name, I will lose my power. But if its name is spoken, it will come."

Solomon then asked, "Which angel stops you?"

The demon replied, "The power of lightning."

Solomon praised God and placed the demon under Beelzeboul's control until another angel, Iax, would come.

Then Solomon summoned another demon. This time, a giant dog appeared and spoke in a loud voice: "Hail, King Solomon!"

Shocked, Solomon asked, "Who are you, and why do you look like a hound?"

The demon replied, "I may look like a dog, but before you were born, I was a man. I was powerful and knew many secrets. I could even control the stars. But now, I harm those who follow after the stars, and I take hold of those who lose control, choking them and leading them to destruction."

Solomon asked the demon, "What is your name?"

The demon replied, "Staff."

Solomon then asked, "What do you do? What powers do you have?"

The demon said, "Send a man with me, and I will take him to the mountains to show him a green stone that moves back and forth. This stone can be used to decorate the Temple of God."

Solomon sent his servant with the demon, giving him a ring with God's seal. "When you find the stone, use this ring to trap the demon, mark the place carefully, and bring the demon back to me," he instructed.

The demon showed the green stone to the servant, who sealed it and brought the demon to Solomon. Solomon then used his ring to bind both the headless demon and the giant hound. He commanded the hound to guard a fiery spirit so that its light could help the workers.

Solomon took 200 shekels of the stone from the mine to support the table of incense, then sealed away the treasure. He ordered the demons to cut marble for the Temple and prayed to God. He then asked the hound, "Which angel weakens you?"

The demon replied, "The great angel Brieus."

Solomon praised God and called for another demon. This time, a roaring lion-like spirit appeared.

The demon said, "I am a spirit that cannot be easily seen. I attack those who are sick, making their bodies weak. But I also have power over other demons. I command legions of them and can drive them out."

Solomon asked, "What is your name?"

The demon replied, "I am called Lion-Bearer."

Solomon then asked, "Which angel can stop you and your demons?"

The demon hesitated. "If I tell you my name, I will also reveal how to defeat all my legions."

Solomon commanded him in the name of God, "Tell me the angel who weakens you."

The demon finally admitted, "It is the one known as Emmanuel, the one who will suffer at the hands of men and cast us into the deep waters."

Hearing this, Solomon praised God and ordered the demon's legion to gather wood. He made the lion-shaped demon cut the wood with his teeth for the Temple's furnace.

Next, Solomon summoned another demon, and a terrifying three-headed dragon appeared.

"Who are you?" Solomon asked.

The demon answered, "I am a spirit of destruction. I cause blindness in unborn babies, make them deaf, and prevent them from speaking. I also strike men so they fall, foam at the mouth, and grind their teeth."

Solomon asked, "Which angel stops you?"

The demon replied, "The one who will one day hang on the cross at the place called 'the head.' That angel defeats me, and I must obey him."

The demon continued, "Where you sit, King Solomon, there is a floating purple column in the air. The demon Ephippas brought it from the Red Sea. He will be captured in a skin bottle and brought to you. Also, there is hidden gold near the entrance of your Temple. If you dig, you will find it."

Solomon sent his servant to check, and everything was just as the demon had said. He sealed the demon with his ring and praised God.

Solomon then asked, "What is your name?"

The demon replied, "I am the crest of dragons."

Solomon commanded him to make bricks for the Temple. The demon had human hands and obeyed.

Then, another demon appeared in the form of a woman, but she had no limbs, only a head with wild, unkempt hair.

Solomon asked, "Who are you?"

She responded, "Why do you want to know? But since you are determined to learn, follow my instructions—go to your storehouse, wash your hands, and sit back on your throne. Then ask me again, and I will tell you who I am."

Solomon did as the demon instructed, holding back his anger because of the wisdom given to him by God. He wanted to hear her story so he could reveal her evil deeds to others. After sitting down, he asked, "Who are you?"

She answered, "I am called Obizuth. I never sleep at night. Instead, I travel all over the world and visit women who are giving birth. I wait for the right moment, and if I succeed, I strangle the newborn child. If I fail, I move on to another place. I never go a night without trying. I am a fierce spirit with many names and forms. I travel from place to place, bringing harm wherever I go. Even though you have sealed me with God's ring, you have not truly captured me. I do only one thing—

destroy children, make them deaf, damage their eyesight, silence their mouths, confuse their minds, and bring pain to their bodies."

Solomon was shocked by her appearance. Her body was covered in darkness, but her eyes glowed bright green. Her wild, dragon-like hair moved as if it were alive, and her voice was loud and clear.

Cleverly, Solomon asked, "Which angel can stop you?"

She replied, "The angel Afarôt, also called Raphael. If someone knows his name and writes it on a woman in childbirth, I cannot enter and harm the child. The number of his name is 640."

Solomon praised God, then ordered that her hair be tied up and that she be hung in front of the Temple for all to see. He wanted the people of Israel to recognize God's power and wisdom through this sign.

Then, Solomon summoned another demon. This one rolled toward him and looked like a dragon, but it had the face and hands of a man. The rest of its body, except for its feet, was like a dragon, and large wings covered its back.

Amazed, Solomon asked, "Who are you? What is your name? Where do you come from?"

The demon answered, "This is the first time I have been captured, King Solomon. People worshipped me as a god, but now your ring and your wisdom from God have defeated me. I am called the Winged Dragon. I do not seek out many women, only the most beautiful ones with a special name connected to my star. I come to them in spirit form and take advantage of them. The children born from this act become spirits of desire. But since humans cannot carry such children, the woman eventually releases them as wind. If you let me go, I will tell you all the secrets of the other demons. But those made of fire will burn up the wood you are collecting for the Temple."

As the demon spoke, Solomon saw fire coming from its mouth, burning up the wood meant for the Temple. He was amazed at its power.

Solomon then asked, "Which angel weakens you?"

The demon replied, "The great angel in the second heaven, called Bazazeth in Hebrew."

After hearing this, Solomon called upon the angel, then ordered the demon to cut marble for the Temple. He thanked God and summoned another spirit.

This time, a female spirit appeared. She had the body of a woman but two extra heads on her shoulders, each with hands.

Solomon asked, "Who are you?"

She answered, "I am Enêpsigos. I have many names."

He asked, "Which angel can defeat you?"

She replied, "Why do you want to know? I change form like the goddess I am called. I shift from one shape to another. But since you are asking, listen carefully. My home is in the moon, and because of that, I have three forms. Sometimes, the wise call me Kronos. Other times, when people summon me, I take a different shape. No one can fully explain or understand me. But I am defeated by the angel Rathanael, who sits in the third heaven. That is why I am speaking to you now. But know this—the Temple you are building cannot contain me."

Solomon prayed to God and called upon the angel Enêpsigos had mentioned. He used his ring to seal her with a triple chain, fastening it beneath her.

Then the spirit prophesied to him, "King Solomon, this is what you are doing to us now. But one day, your kingdom will fall. This Temple will be destroyed by the King of Persia, the Medes, and the Chaldeans. The sacred objects you make will be taken and used for false gods. The jars where you have trapped demons will be broken, and we will be set free. We will spread throughout the world, misleading people for a long time. But when the Son of God is stretched upon a cross, we will finally be defeated. There will be no other king like Him. He will stop all of us, and even the first devil will try to tempt Him but fail. The number of His name is 644, and He is Emmanuel. Because of this, King Solomon, your time is short, and your kingdom will not last. It will be given to your servant."

After hearing this, Solomon praised God. Even though the demons had warned him of the future, he didn't believe them at first. But when their words came true, he understood. Before he died, he wrote this account for the people of Israel so they would know about the demons, their powers, and the names of the angels that could defeat them. He gave thanks to God and ordered the spirits to be bound with unbreakable chains.

Then, Solomon summoned another demon. This one had the front body of a horse but the tail of a fish. It had a powerful voice and said,"King Solomon, I am a powerful sea spirit, obsessed with gold and silver. I travel through the waters, creating massive waves that overturn ships. I trick sailors by turning into a wave and crashing into them. I don't crave human bodies, but I throw people out of the sea to serve my own purpose. Beelzebul, who rules over demons in the air and underground, shares power with us. That is why I left the sea to meet with him."

The demon continued, "I can also take human form, and people call me Kunospaston. This name fits because I make people feel weak and sick when I approach them. I went to speak with Beelzebul, but he captured me and brought me here. Now I stand before you, unable to escape because of your ring. In two or three days, I will grow weaker since I cannot survive without water."

Solomon asked, "Which angel can defeat you?"

The demon answered, "Iameth."

Solomon praised God and ordered the demon to be sealed inside a container with ten jugs of seawater. He sealed it with his ring and placed it inside the Temple. Then, he summoned another spirit.

A new demon appeared, shaped like a man but with glowing eyes. It carried a sharp blade.

Solomon asked, "Who are you?"

The demon answered, "I am a spirit of lust, born from the remains of a giant who died in battle."

Solomon asked, "What do you do on earth, and where do you live?"

The demon replied, "I stay in places full of life, but I wait in cemeteries, disguised as the dead. When people pass by, I attack them with my sword. If I fail, I possess them, making them harm themselves. Their hair falls out, and they waste away."

Solomon warned him, "Fear the God of heaven and earth. Tell me which angel weakens you."

The demon answered, "The one who will become the Savior. If anyone writes His number on their forehead, I will flee in fear."

Solomon praised God and locked the demon away.

Then, he summoned another group of spirits. This time, thirty-six demons appeared. They had human bodies but animal heads—some looked like dogs, donkeys, oxen, and birds.

Solomon asked, "Who are you?"

The demons spoke as one: "We are the thirty-six rulers of darkness. But since God has given you power over all spirits, we appear before you willingly. We come from the signs of the zodiac—Ram, Bull, Twins, Crab, Lion, Virgin, Scales, Scorpion, Archer, Goat, Water-Pourer, and Fish."

Solomon called upon God and asked each one to describe its powers.

The first spirit said, "I am the first of the zodiac, the Ram. My name is Ruax. I make people feel lazy and cloud their minds. But if someone says, 'Michael, imprison Ruax,' I will flee."

The second said, "I am Barsafael. I cause migraines. If someone calls upon Gabriel to imprison me, I will retreat."

The third said, "I am Arôtosael. I harm people's eyes and make them weak. If someone says, 'Uriel, imprison Arôtosael,' I will leave."

The fourth said, "I am Iudal. I make people lose their hearing. If someone calls Uruel against me, I will retreat."

The fifth said, "I am Sphendonaêl. I cause swelling in the throat and make people sick. If someone prays to Sabrael, I will flee."

The sixth said, "I am Sphandôr. I weaken people's shoulders, paralyze their hands, and make their bones brittle. If someone says, 'Araêl, imprison Sphandôr,' I will leave."

The seventh said, "I am Belbel. I fill people's hearts and minds with confusion. If someone calls on Araêl to imprison me, I will disappear."

The eighth said, "I am Kurtaêl. I cause stomach pain and cramping. If someone calls on Iaôth, I will flee."

The ninth said, "I am Metathiax. I make people's kidneys ache. If someone calls upon Adônaêl, I will retreat."

The tenth said, "I am Katanikotaêl. I bring conflict into homes and make people argue. If someone writes the names of the angels Iae, Ieô, and Sabaôth on seven laurel leaves, washes them in water, and sprinkles their house, I will leave."

The eleventh said, "I am Saphathoraél. I cause people to take sides against each other and lead them into foolish arguments. If someone writes the names of the angels Iacô, Iealô, Iôelet, and Sabaôth on a piece of paper, folds it up, and keeps it near them, I will retreat."

Solomon listened to each demon and sealed them with his ring. Then, he gave them tasks to help build the Temple.

The thirteenth spirit said, "My name is Bobel, and I cause nerve diseases. If someone says, 'Adonael, imprison Bothothel,' I will leave immediately."

The fourteenth said, "I am Kumeatel. I bring chills and numbness. If someone says, 'Zoroel, imprison Kumeatel,' I will go away."

The fifteenth said, "I am Roeled. I cause cold, frost, and stomach pain. If someone says, 'Iax, do not stay, do not be warmed, for Solomon is fairer than eleven fathers,' I will leave right away."

The sixteenth said, "I am Atrax. I give people fevers that are dangerous and hard to cure. To stop me, mix coriander and spread it on the lips while saying, 'Fever from filth, I command you by the throne of the highest God, leave the filth and leave God's creation.' Then I will disappear."

The seventeenth said, "I am Ieropael. I sit on people's stomachs and cause seizures, whether they are at home or walking outside. If someone whispers into their right ear three times the names 'Iudarize, Sabune, Deno,' I will leave."

The eighteenth said, "I am Buldumech. I create fights between husbands and wives. If someone writes down the names of your ancestors, Solomon, on paper and places it in the entrance of their home, I will leave. The message should say: 'The God of Abraham, the God of Isaac, and the God of Jacob commands you to leave this house in peace.' Then I will go away."

The nineteenth said, "I am Naoth. I sit on people's knees. If someone writes on paper, 'Phnunoboeol, depart Nathath, and do not touch the neck,' I will leave immediately."

The twentieth said, "I am Mardero. I cause deadly fevers. If someone writes on a book page, 'Sphener, Rafael, leave me, do not harm me,' and ties it around their neck, I will disappear."

The twenty-first said, "I am Alath. I make children cough and struggle to breathe. If someone writes on paper, 'Rorex, chase away Alath,' and ties it around the child's neck, I will leave."

The twenty-third said, "I am Nefthada. I cause kidney pain and make it hard for people to urinate. If someone writes on a tin plate, 'Iathoth, Uruel, Nephthada,' and ties it around their waist, I will leave."

The twenty-fourth said, "I am Akton. I cause pain in the ribs and lower back. If someone carves on a piece of copper taken from a shipwreck the words 'Marmaraoth, Sabaoth, chase away Akton' and ties it around their waist, I will go away."

The twenty-fifth said, "I am Anatreth. I cause burning fevers inside people's bodies. If someone says, 'Arara, Charara,' I will leave immediately."

The twenty-sixth said, "I am Enenuth. I confuse people's minds, change their hearts, and make them lose their teeth. If someone writes, 'Allazool, chase away Enenuth,' and ties it around themselves, I will go away."

The twenty-seventh said, "I am Pheth. I cause weight loss and bleeding. If someone mixes my name into sweet, unmixed wine and says, 'I command you by the eleventh aeon to stop, I demand, Pheth (Axiopheth),' and gives it to the sick person to drink, I will leave."

The twenty-eighth said, "I am Harpax. I cause sleeplessness. If someone writes 'Kokphnedismos' and ties it around their head, I will leave."

The twenty-ninth said, "I am Anoster. I cause problems in the womb and bladder pain. If someone grinds three laurel seeds into pure oil, rubs it on themselves, and says, 'I command you, Anoster, stop by Marmarao,' I will disappear."

The thirtieth said, "I am Alleborith. If someone swallows a fishbone, they must take another fishbone, cough, and I will leave."

The thirty-first said, "I am Hephesimireth. I cause long-lasting diseases. If someone rubs salt in their hand, mixes it with oil, and says, 'Seraphim, Cherubim, help me!' I will go away."

The thirty-second said, "I am Ichthion. I paralyze muscles and cause bruising. If someone says, 'Adonaeth, help!' I will leave."

The thirty-third said, "I am Agchonion. I hide in baby blankets and dangerous cliffs. If someone writes the name 'Lycurgos' on fig leaves, removing one letter at a time, I will disappear."

The thirty-fourth said, "I am Autothith. I cause fights and anger. I am stopped if someone writes 'Alpha and Omega.'"

The thirty-fifth said, "I am Phthenoth. I cast an evil eye on people. If someone draws an eye with suffering, I am stopped."

The thirty-sixth said, "I am Bianakith. I attack people's bodies, ruin homes, and cause flesh to rot. If someone writes 'Melto, Ardu, Anaath' on their front door, I will leave."

After hearing all of this, Solomon praised the God of heaven and earth. He commanded the spirits to bring water to the Temple and prayed that all harmful demons would be captured and brought to him. Some of the demons were forced to work on building the Temple, while others were locked away. Some were assigned to work with fire, making gold and silver, while others were placed in different prisons.

Solomon lived in peace, ruling over all the earth. He finished building the Temple of God, and his kingdom was successful. Jerusalem was safe and joyful. Kings from all over the world came to see the Temple and to hear Solomon's wisdom. They brought gifts of gold, silver, gemstones, bronze, iron, lead, and wood that would not decay to help furnish the Temple.

Among them was the queen of the South, a powerful sorceress. She bowed before Solomon, listened to his wisdom, and praised the God of Israel. She tested Solomon with many questions, and he taught her with all the knowledge he had received from God. The people of Israel praised God.

One day, an old man who worked on the Temple came to Solomon and bowed. He said, "King Solomon, have mercy on me. I am an old man, and my only son mistreats me. He insults me, pulls my hair, and threatens my life. Please, punish him for me."

Solomon looked at the old man with pity and ordered his son to be brought before him. When the young man arrived, Solomon asked if the accusations were true. The son said, "I am not so foolish as to hit my own father. Please, my king, do not believe such a terrible thing about me."

Solomon asked the old man to reconsider and accept his son's apology, but the father refused and wanted him to be punished. Just as Solomon was about to make his judgment, he saw the demon Ornias laughing. This made Solomon angry, and he ordered everyone else to leave so he could question Ornias.

When the demon was brought before him, Solomon asked, "Why did you laugh in my presence, cursed one?"

Ornias replied, "King, I wasn't laughing at you. I laughed because of this poor old man and his foolish son. In three days, the son will die unexpectedly, and the father is trying to have him killed for no reason."

When I heard this, I asked the demon, "Are you telling the truth?" The demon replied, "Yes, King." After hearing that, I had the demon taken away and brought the old man and his son before me again. I told them to make peace with each other, gave them food, and told the old man, "Bring your son back to me in three days, and I will take care of him." They bowed and left.

After they left, I called for Ornias and asked, "How do you know this will happen?" He answered, "We demons fly up to the sky and move among the stars. We hear the decisions made about people's lives, and then we come down and carry out those fates—sometimes through illness, fire, accidents, or violence. If a person does not die suddenly, we take on human form so that people worship us as gods."

When I heard this, I praised God. Then I asked him, "How can demons enter heaven and mix with the stars and angels?" He answered, "Just as events happen in heaven, they also happen on earth. There are rulers and powers in both places. We demons fly through the air and hear the voices of heavenly beings, but we have no place to rest. We lose strength and fall from the sky like leaves from a tree. When people see this, they think stars are falling, but it is really us. We fall like lightning at night, suddenly crashing to the ground. Sometimes, we set cities on fire or burn fields. But the stars in heaven are fixed, just like the sun and the moon."

I ordered the demon to be locked away for five days. When the time passed, I called the old man back. He arrived looking sad, with a sorrowful expression. I asked, "Where is your son? Why do you look like this?" He answered, "My son has died, and I have been sitting at his grave. He has been gone for two days now." When I heard this, I realized Ornias had told the truth, and I praised the God of Israel.

The queen of the South saw all of this and was amazed. She praised the God of Israel and watched as the Temple was being built. She gave a large amount of gold, silver, and bronze and entered the Temple. She admired the incense altar, the metal supports, the glowing gemstones, the golden lampstands, and the colorful decorations. She marveled at the golden pillars and all the beautiful materials, aside from the demons who had been forced to work. There was peace in my kingdom and throughout the land.

One day, I received a letter from King Adares of Arabia. It said:

"King Solomon, greetings. We have heard of your great wisdom, which comes from the Lord. We know that you have power over spirits in the air, on the earth, and under the ground. There is a terrible spirit in Arabia that appears as a strong wind every morning until midday. It is deadly and kills both people and animals. No one can survive against this demon. We ask for your help, wise king, to use the knowledge given to you by God to capture this spirit. If you do this, we and all our people will serve you. All of Arabia will live in peace with you if you save us. Please do not ignore our request, or our land will be destroyed. We beg for your help. Farewell, great king."

After reading the letter, I folded it up and told my people, "Remind me of this letter in seven days." Meanwhile, the Temple was being completed. A special stone was chosen for the Temple's cornerstone, and the workers and demons tried to move it into place, but it was too heavy for them. No one was strong enough to lift it.

After seven days, I remembered the letter from the Arabian king. I called a servant and told him, "Take a camel, a leather flask, and this ring. Travel to Arabia and find the place where the wind blows. Hold the flask open with the ring in front of it. When the wind fills the flask, you will know the demon is inside. Quickly seal the flask shut and bring it back to me. If the demon offers you gold or silver in exchange for its freedom, do not be tempted. Instead, make it tell you where treasure is hidden, then mark those places and seal them with this ring. Bring the demon to me safely. Now go, and may you be protected."

The servant obeyed my orders. When he arrived, the Arabs doubted that he could capture the demon. But when morning came, he stood before the wind, opened the flask, and held the ring over its opening. The demon, not realizing the trap, blew into the flask and got trapped inside. The servant quickly sealed it in the name of the Lord. The demon could no longer harm the city. The servant stayed there for three days to make sure the wind did not return, and the people of Arabia saw that he had captured the spirit.

The servant tied the flask to his camel and was sent off with great honor, receiving many gifts. He brought the flask to the Temple and placed it in the center. The next day, when I entered the Temple, the flask moved on its own, rolling forward seven steps before bowing before me. I was amazed that the demon still had power while trapped inside. I commanded it to stand up, and the flask rose into the air.

I asked, "Who are you?"

The demon inside answered, "I am called Ephippas, the spirit of Arabia."

I asked, "Is that your true name?"

The demon said, "Yes. Wherever I wish, I land, start fires, and bring death."

I asked, "Which angel has power over you?"

The demon replied, "The one true God, who will be born of a virgin and be crucified by the Jews. The angels and archangels worship Him. He weakens me and takes away my strength, which my father, the devil, gave me."

I asked, "What are you capable of?"

The demon answered, "I can move mountains, make kings break their oaths, and cause trees to wither and lose their leaves."

I asked, "Can you lift this heavy stone and place it in the Temple?"

The demon replied, "Not only can I lift it, but with the help of the demon who controls the Red Sea, I can bring the great pillar of air and set it in Jerusalem."

I commanded him to prove it. The flask lost its air, and I placed it under the stone. The demon lifted the stone and carried it up the Temple steps, placing it in the exact spot needed. When I saw this, I remembered the scripture that says, "The stone the builders rejected has become the cornerstone." I knew that it was not by my power but by God's will that the demon had placed the stone.

Ephippas then brought another demon from the Red Sea, carrying a great pillar. I tricked the demons so they would not shake the entire earth with their power. I sealed them with my ring, and they swore, "As long as the Lord lives, we will hold up this pillar until the end of time. But when the pillar falls, the world will end."

I praised God and continued decorating the Temple. My kingdom was peaceful, and I had everything I desired. I took many wives from different lands, and I led my army to conquer the Jebusites. There, I saw a woman I fell in love with and wanted to marry her. I asked the priests to allow me to marry her, but they said, "If you want to marry her, you must first worship our gods, Raphan and Moloch."

I refused, saying, "I will not worship false gods." But they told the woman not to be with me unless I sacrificed to their gods. I struggled with this, but she tricked me. She gave me five grasshoppers and told me, "Crush these in the name of Moloch, and I will be with you." I foolishly did as she said, and at that moment, the Spirit of God left me. I became weak and foolish. She then convinced me to build temples for false gods like Baal, Raphan, and Moloch.

I, in my foolishness, followed her wishes, and God's presence left me. My spirit became dark, and I was led astray by idols and demons. That is why I wrote this testament—for those who read it to learn from my mistakes. Focus on what truly matters in the end, not the foolishness of the past, so that you may find God's grace forever. Amen.

Thank You for Reading

Dear Reader,

We hope this timeless classic has sparked your imagination and enriched your literary journey. Now that you've turned the final page, we want to share a vision for the future of reading—one where every classic you've ever wanted to explore is at your fingertips, in a format that best suits your life.

We'd like to invite you to gain immediate, unlimited digital & audiobook access to hundreds of the most treasured literary classics ever written—along with the option to secure deluxe paperback, hardcover & box set editions at printing cost. Together, we can spark a new global literary renaissance alongside our small, independent publishing house called "The Library of Alexandria."

Thousands of years ago, the Library of Alexandria stood as a beacon of knowledge—until it was lost to history. We aim to reignite that spirit of preservation and discovery right now, in the modern age—only this time, it's accessible to all, in every language and every format.

Picture a world where every timeless classic, novel, poem, or philosophical treatise is not only available to read but also updated for today's readers—modernized, translated into any language or dialect, and ready to enjoy in any format you choose, whether that is in an eBook, audiobook, paperback, or deluxe hardcover & box set version a printing cost.

By joining our movement to rebuild the modern Library of Alexandria, you become part of an unprecedented mission to offer:

- **Unlimited Audiobook & eBook Access to the Greatest Classics of All Time**

  Instantly explore thousands of legendary works, from Plato and Shakespeare to Jane Austen and Leo Tolstoy. All are instantly ready to read or listen to, giving you a complete literary universe at your fingertips.

- **Paperback & Deluxe Editions at Printing Costs:**

  Purchase any title in a paperback, deluxe hardbound, or deluxe boxset edition at printing costs, shipped right to your doorstep. Curate your personal library of Alexandria with editions worthy of display—crafted to last, designed to captivate, and delivered straight to your door.

- **Modern translations for Contemporary Readers in all languages and dialects**

  Discover a vast selection of classics reimagined in clear, current language—no more struggling with outdated phrases or obscure references. Next to the original versions, we aim to offer translations in as many languages and dialects as possible.

  As we continue our translation efforts and add new languages, readers everywhere can connect with these works as if they were written today. By bridging linguistic divides, you're contributing to ensuring that these timeless stories become more meaningful, accessible, and inspiring for people across the globe.

- **Your Personal Library of Alexandria:**

  Over the months and years, you'll curate a unique physical archive of classics—each volume a testament to your taste, curiosity, and love of knowledge. It's not just about owning books—it's about curating a cultural legacy you'll cherish and pass down for generations to come.

- **Join a Global Literary Renaissance:**

  Your support fuels an ongoing mission: allowing us to reinvest in offering deluxe print editions (including special boxsets) at their true cost, broaden the range of available formats and translations, and extend the reach of these works to new audiences worldwide. By joining today, you're not just preserving a legacy of masterpieces; you set in motion a powerful wave of literary accessibility.

  We are more than a publisher—we're a movement, and we can't do it alone. Your support lets us scale our mission, preserving and reimagining history's greatest works for tomorrow's readers.

Become a Torchbearer of knowledge.

Thank you for picking up this book and allowing us into your literary journey. As you turn the pages, know that you're part of something larger: a global effort to keep these stories alive, share their wisdom across borders and generations, and spark a true cultural revival for the modern era.

If this resonates with you—please consider taking the next step by visiting:

www.libraryofalexandria.com

With gratitude and a shared love of knowledge,

The Modern Library of Alexandria Team

Visit:

www.libraryofalexandria.com

Or scan the code below:

www.ingramcontent.com/pod-product-compliance
Lightning Source LLC
Chambersburg PA
CBHW011203090426
42742CB00019B/3395

9 781804 217450